ALSO BY AZAR NAFISI

Reading Lolita in Tehran

Things I've Been Silent About

Bibi e la Voce Verde (in Italian, a children's story)

The Republic of Imagination

That Other World

READ DA

READ
DANGEROUSLY

THE SUBVERSIVE POWER OF LITERATURE
IN TROUBLED TIMES

AZAR NAFISI

DEY ST.
An Imprint of WILLIAM MORROW

HarperCollins books may be purchased for educational, business, or sales promotional use. For information, please email the Special Markets Department at SPsales@harpercollins.com.

FIRST EDITION

Designed by Michelle Crowe

Library of Congress Cataloging-in-Publication Data has been applied for.

ISBN 978-0-06-294736-9

22 23 24 25 26   LSC   10 9 8 7 6 5 4 3 2 1

As always, to my family, Bijan, Negar, and Dara Naderi. And my grandchildren, Cyrus Colman Naderi and Iliana Nafisi Guedenis. And in memory of Bryce Nafisi Naderi.

Create dangerously, for people who read dangerously. This is what I've always thought it meant to be a writer. Writing, knowing in part that no matter how trivial your words may seem, someday, somewhere, someone may risk his or her life to read them.

Create Dangerously: The Immigrant Artist at Work
—Edwidge Danticat

CONTENTS

AUTHOR'S NOTE

I SEE THIS, IN MANY WAYS, as the closing title in a quartet of books, which, setting aside my memoir (*Things I've Been Silent About*), began with *That Other World*, *Reading Lolita in Tehran*, and *The Republic of Imagination*. Like those books, *Read Dangerously* draws upon my lived experiences, in both Iran and the United States. As such, readers who are familiar with my other work may recognize some of the broad biographical contours of my story, though their purpose in this book is quite different.

READ DANGEROUSLY

INTRODUCTION

When a reader falls in love with a book, it leaves its essence inside him, like radioactive fallout in an arable field, and after that there are certain crops that will no longer grow in him, while other, stranger, more fantastic growths may occasionally be produced.

—Salman Rushdie

ON OCTOBER 8, 2016, I sat down and wrote a letter to my father, who had been dead for twelve years. I know the date because I noted in my letter that it was the day after the *Washington Post* published the lewd conversation between Billy Bush and Donald Trump in which Trump boasted about grabbing women's genitals.

During his lifetime, it was not unusual for me to exchange letters with my father. He first wrote me when I was four, in a diary addressed only to me, which, after his death, I discovered among his letters and diaries. I first wrote to him when I was six, while he was in America studying. I jotted down a few words on scraps of paper torn from my notebook, addressing him as Baba jan, the equivalent of "dearest Dad" in Persian, and signing off the letter with "Baba's daughter." We wrote not just when one of us was traveling, but also while we lived in the same country—even when we lived in the same house.

We wrote each other long letters on important occasions: when I was sent to England at the age of thirteen to continue my studies, or when my father, then the mayor of Tehran, was jailed for political reasons in 1963—because he would not obey his archenemies, the prime minister and the minister of the interior. We exchanged letters when he was finally exonerated of all charges, after having spent four years in what was called a temporary jail. We exchanged letters about my first wedding, at the age of eighteen, which he, being in jail, could not attend, and I continued to write from the University of Oklahoma, which I attended along with my first husband. My father was the first person I wrote to about my unhappy marriage and the decision to divorce, and, a few years later, about my second husband, Bijan, and my decision to marry him.

I graduated college and continued on for a PhD, which I completed right after the Islamic Revolution in 1979. I returned to Iran to teach but was expelled from the university for refusing to wear the mandatory veil. My father and I wrote about all of this, of course. We wrote when my daughter, Negar, and my son, Dara, were born. When I migrated back to America in July 1997, we exchanged long faxes in which we discussed everything from the most personal to the political and the intellectual: how lucky it was that my husband and I and our children lived in Washington, DC, the same city where some of my closest friends, and my kind and generous sisters-in-law, lived with their families; how exhilarating it was to watch uncensored movies and read uncensored books; how much I missed him. We wrote about the excitement of my new work, the books we each read, the lessons to be learned from Gandhi, Dr. Martin Luther King Jr., and Montaigne. He created a list of the great works of Iranian literature for me to pass down to my children "so that they will remember Iran," he said. We discussed the books I taught in my classes, as well as America's evasion of reality and its growing obsession with comfort and entertainment. I wrote to him when I was happy, I wrote to him when I was unhappy, I wrote to him when I was excited, I wrote to him when I was angry or depressed.

On that day in October, I wrote because I was depressed, thinking of the two countries I called home. In Iran, the theocracy was in full force; despite people's intense dissatisfaction and consistent protests, nothing had changed. The ayatollahs continued to harass, jail, torture, and kill innocent citizens. In America, although vastly different from Iran, the society was fast becoming polarized—too much ideology and not enough discourse—in some instances reminding me of the Islamic Republic. My father and I had many exchanges about how to deal with our oppressors, with those we call not just adversary but enemy. His imprisonment and those responsible for it were the topic of many conversations over the years, and, later, a revolution and a war made it almost a daily preoccupation.

And now, in America, I returned to the same question, finding it so central to the preservation of democracy. I wrote my father that I felt tongue-tied thinking of Trump's candidacy, not just because of his person but also because of what he represented and revealed about us. I wrote him that in the Trump era we are preoccupied by our enemies, real or manufactured, that most of our actions are reactions to these real or fabricated enemies. I also told father that I missed him: "As we say in Persian, your place is empty." His place had never been this empty.

I wrote how, all my life, I felt I had been his number one defender, confidante, friend, and fellow conspirator, despite our times of anger, or feelings of betrayal and bitterness. I said, "At times, I was hard on you, in the same hard way I loved you. But now death and distance have brought out the other feelings, the ones I evoke when I return to the happiest moments of my childhood: the storytelling."

Like all loving and intimate relationships, ours had its ups and downs, but there was one aspect of our bond that remained unsullied: the stories he told me each night during my childhood. When my father would sit down to tell me some of my favorite stories, the unexpected joy was like a brief electric shock. I knew instinctively, even when I was very young, that the moment was sacred, I was being offered something precious and rare: the key to a secret world.

He was democratic in choosing the stories. One night he would tell the tales from our epic poet Ferdowsi's book *Shahnameh* (*The Book of Kings*); the next night, we would travel to France with the Little Prince; the night after that, to England with Alice. Then to Denmark with the Little Match Girl, to Turkey with Mullah Nassreddin, to America with Charlotte and her web, or to Italy with Pinocchio. He brought the whole world into my little room. Time and again as a teenager, and later as a college student, a teacher, a writer, an activist, a mother, I would return to that room to draw upon the strength of those stories.

I left Iran for the first time at the age of thirteen to continue my education in England, and, ever since, books and stories have been my talismans, my portable home, the only home I could rely on, the only home I knew would never betray me, the only home I could never be forced to leave. Reading and writing have protected me through the worst moments of my life, through loneliness, terror, doubt, and anxiety. And they have also given me new eyes with which to see both my homeland and my adopted country.

In Iran, like all totalitarian states, the regime pays too much attention to poets and writers, harassing, jailing, and even killing them. The problem in America is that too little attention is paid to them. They are silenced not by torture and jail but by indifference and negligence. I am reminded of James Baldwin's claim that "Neither love nor terror makes one blind: indifference makes one blind." In the United States, it is mainly we, the people, who are the problem; we who take the existence of challenging literature for granted, or see reading as solely a comfort, seeking out only texts that confirm our presuppositions and prejudices. Perhaps for us, the very idea of change is dangerous, and what we avoid is reading dangerously.

AUTHORS ARE NOT INFALLIBLE. Each great writer is the child of her or his age, certainly. But the miraculous aspect of great books is their ability to both reflect and transcend the prejudices of the author as well as their time and place. It is this quality that allows a young woman in twentieth-century Iran to read a Greek man named Aeschylus, who lived thousands of years ago, and to empathize with him. Reading does not necessarily lead to direct political action, but it fosters a mindset that questions and doubts; that is not content with the establishment or the established. Fiction arouses our curiosity, and it is this curiosity, this restlessness, this desire to know that makes both writing and reading so dangerous.

Over the years, I have been saying how the structure of great fiction is based on multivocality, on a democracy of different perspectives where even the villain has a voice, while bad fiction reduces all voices to one voice, that of the writer, who, like a dictator, stifles all the characters in order to impose his message and agenda. Great works of literature—works that are truly *dangerous*—question and expose that dictatorial impulse, both on the page and in the public space. As I sat down to write my father on that day in October, reading dangerously had never felt more important.

WE ARE LIVING IN A post-Trump era, but Trump will be with us for a long time; if not physically, then figuratively, representing the autocratic mindset and tendencies within a democracy. We will experience the aftershocks of his presidency in the years to come. The establishment of some form of normalcy does not mean that these deep undercurrents of hatred have gone away and democracy is safe. This era is overwhelmed by violence both in rhetoric and reality, communicating not through inclusion but elimination. Adversaries and opponents are now reduced to and defined as enemies. This era is also dominated by lies. Unlike fiction that seeks the truth, lies are based on illusions that are mistaken for reality. But we also live in a time of hope and transition, where there is a real opportunity for change, for genuine equality, for democracy. It all depends on what we choose and how we choose to implement it.

How do we confront the current crisis? How do we genuinely change? Autocratic tendencies remind us that what we need to fight and change are not merely political positions or policies, but *attitudes*, a way of looking at and acting in the world. It is ironic that in opposing them, in trying not to be like them, we discover our own values as well as our own flaws and our negligence in defense of those values. For surely we too must share the blame—through passivity or inadvertent complicity—in creating the problems that face us today.

We in this country have lost the art of engaging with the opposition. This is where reading dangerously comes in: it teaches us how to deal with the enemy. We need to know not just how to deal with friends and allies, but with adversaries and enemies as well. Knowing your enemy involves discovering yourself. Democracy depends upon engagement with our adversaries and opponents. It depends upon us being made to think, and rethink, assess and reassess our own positions, face both the enemies outside of us and the ones within. I like what Jonathan Chait says in a 2021 piece in

New York magazine about the Republican Party demoting Wyoming congresswoman Liz Cheney for having the "audacity" to not tow the party line regarding Trump's actions before and during the US Capitol riots of January 6, 2021: "You make peace with your enemies, not your friends."

WHEN I WAS A CHILD, and Father wanted to explain something complicated to me, he would try to make me understand it through telling me a story. As I tried to make my father understand our present moment, I drew inspiration from this. More and more, I found myself writing to my father about books. It is now my turn to tell him my stories.

My letters are focused on the events that shaped our lives through a crucial and turbulent time in recent history, beginning with the bloody November 2019 protests that rocked the Islamic Republic of Iran, and ending with the protests over the killing of George Floyd in America during the summer of 2020. I believe these events encapsulate not just what was happening then but also what is happening now and will happen in the foreseeable future.

I spent the four years of Trump's presidency reading, rereading, and reflecting on works of fiction about trauma, both personal and political. Through these books, which came to form the backbone of my letters to my father, I attempted to make sense of our present moment—to use their stories to explain something complicated about America to him.

I began, as so much American writing these past four years has, with the allure and the dire threat of totalitarianism, tracing this idea from Plato's *Republic* through to Ray Bradbury's *Fahrenheit 451* and Salman Rushdie's *Satanic Verses*. This era has laid bare the clash between the poet and the tyrant—and the precarious place a writer, or, for that matter, a reader occupies within an absolutist society. I then moved on to two great writers of twentieth-century letters, Zora Neale Hurston and Toni Morrison, whose novels offer commentary on the big political themes of our day—race, gender, oppression—as incisive as any being written today.

Next, I found myself writing about war, for this century and the previous one have been full of them: against nations, against people, people against people, and, in 2020, against a viral pandemic. David Grossman, Elliot Ackerman, and Elias Khoury were my touchstones here; they expose the dehumanization and hatred that are intrinsic parts of war. As the United States lurched through the first months of a turbulent 2020, it began to feel a bit like Margaret Atwood's Republic of Gilead, so she too features prominently in this exchange with my father. And I closed with a source of inspiration for this book, namely, James Baldwin, and a contemporary writer who shares some of his sensibilities, Ta-Nehisi Coates, as I attempted to understand the murder of George Floyd and the protests that followed.

This is how the idea for this book gradually took shape. My letters became a meditation, both personal and political, through the eyes of imagination, especially about my migrant experience and my two homes, Iran and the United States. It also revisited some of the facts and events in my previous writing, placing them in a new light and context. Its focus is on a specific mindset: an absolutist one that allows no room for dialogue or change of mind, that sees everyone in the opposition or different as an enemy. This mindset is best manifested in totalitarian systems, but it exists in democracies as well.

The aim of this book is to involve the reader and make her an active participant in thinking about these questions: How do

we deal with feelings of frustration and anger in the face of abso-
lutism? How do we confront the lies and replace them with the
truth? How do we resist injustice and avoid becoming paralyzed
by fantasies of revenge? How do we become just toward those who
have been unjust to us? How do we deal with our enemy without
either becoming like him or surrendering to him?

I turn to fiction because responding to these questions, and
dealing with our adversaries, first and foremost requires understanding, and for that we need the imaginative power that fiction cultivates. In fiction, as in real life, plot moves forward and
character is developed through opposition and conflict. Personal,
political, or literary opposition can always find a form. And I am
interested here to explore the different forms and shapes both
literary and actual opposition take that can lead to a change in
perspective. Because change is difficult to effect, and differences
often seem insurmountable, and literature teaches us how we are
compelled to act in certain ways, leading us to the question "How
do we change the world?" followed by "How do we change ourselves?"

The writers in this book have lived on the edge of trauma and
danger and have found literature and imagination not only important but, in fact, vital to their well-being. For them, writing
was a way of surviving—in a sense, their only way of surviving.
It should be clear by now that when I talk about books, I am not
talking about literature of resistance but *literature as resistance*. I
am interested in ways through which literature and art resist seats
of power—not only that of kings and tyrants, but the tyrant within
us as well. It is possible to change policies, but it is far more difficult to change attitudes. My goal in this book, as in all the books
I have written, is to replace the rifts created by politics with con-
nections gained through imagination.

Right now books are in danger. One can go a step further and say that imagination and ideas are in danger, and whenever they are threatened, we know that our reality is similarly in danger. Remember the saying "First they burn books, then they kill people"? This is a good time to remember what Toni Morrison once said: ". . . art takes us and makes us take a journey beyond price, beyond cost, into bearing witness to the world as it is and as it should be."

RUSHDIE, PLATO, BRADBURY

NOVEMBER 22–DECEMBER 24, 2019

Dearest Baba,

How I wish you were here. Especially here, in Washington, DC, the city I first heard about because of you. I wonder how much has changed and how much has remained the same since the fifties, when you lived in DC on a government grant while working on your master's degree at the American University. I had seen the photos and heard about the beautiful city from you. The Washington of your photos was an expanse of green. There you were, sitting picnic style with friends on a green lawn or standing in the shadow of a tall ancient tree.

I live in the vicinity of the city's historic Foggy Bottom area. When I am asked where I live, I love saying with a British accent, "Foggy Bottom"! I think you would have appreciated the place. I am surrounded by American icons representing the best and the worst. My apartment is a few minutes from the Kennedy Center, and if I stand in the middle of Virginia Ave., I can see the Washington Monument. Then there is the notorious Watergate building, reminder of Nixon, and

Clinton's Monica Lewinsky scandals. Later, Condoleezza Rice lived there, as did my favorite Supreme Court justice, Ruth Bader Ginsburg.

But most of all, I think you would have appreciated the river. The window in our living room opens to the balcony and the Potomac below, and almost every morning, I look out and salute it. This river plays the same function for me that Mount Damavand did in Tehran. You remember our living room window held a view of that historic mountain. Ever since I was a child, I've heard so much about Damavand. I remember you saying that it is at the heart of Persian mythology and culture, a symbol of national pride—you can go back more than a thousand years and find it in the lines of our great epic poet Ferdowsi. I heard of Damavand in the stories you told me from *Shahnameh*, Ferdowsi's opus that begins with Persian mythology and ancient pre-Islamic history, and ends with the Arab conquest of Persia in the seventh century.

In Ferdowsi's stories, Damavand is a symbol of resistance against, and triumph over, despotic rulers and foreign invaders. I so well remember the story of Zahhak, perhaps the most hated of these rulers, who feeds the two serpents sprouting from his shoulders with the brains of Persian youth. Each time I heard the story, I would feel immense relief when Zahhak is finally defeated by Prince Fereydun, who, with the help of Kaveh the blacksmith, binds and chains him in a cave underneath Damavand.

At school, we learned that Damavand was the third highest peak in the world. Recently, I have researched the mountain, and I do not find that fact anywhere. It is instead number twelve, though it is also the highest mountain peak in Iran

and the second highest volcano in Asia after Mount Everest.
I didn't know Damavand was an active volcano. Is this the
reason there is always a misty halo surrounding its peak?

The Potomac also plays an important role in the history
and story of America. It is called the "nation's river," probably
because it was the site of many skirmishes between the Union
and the Confederacy during the Civil War. Indeed, the largest
Union army was named after it. George Washington was born
and lived in the Potomac basin. The river, like the mountain, is
important to me. They signify beauty and endurance, link the
city to nature, and remind us that the mountain and the river
were here before us and will be here after we are gone.

This mix of history and nature means a great deal to me,
as it did to you. I first learned of Damavand from you. Do you
remember the long walks we took through the streets of Tehran
together, you telling me stories and keeping me going with
promises of ice cream and bookshops? The city, surrounded by
the mountains and filled with promises and secrets, became
magical to me. Even as an adult, I so loved walking those streets
to relieve my anxieties. Washington also has beautiful streets
and parks, as you know. I roam around the city, sometimes
wondering if you had walked these same steps. How I miss our
lively conversations during those so long ago walks. I follow
the bends of the Potomac and think about Damavand. They
represent the best that each of my two homes has offered me.

IF YOU COULD BE HERE, we would have walked to the waterfront,
discussing people, projects, and ideas. You always enjoyed
exchanging ideas. Since you are not here, I have to imagine

you walking by my side. Maybe we would stop by the National
Portrait Gallery to take a look at those who made this country
what it is, not just the ones you know and talk about in your
writing, but those I don't think you know about, like a fellow
called Benjamin Lay (1682–1759), a Quaker and a dedicated
abolitionist. He was morally consistent in his defense of the
enslaved people, too strident even for the abolitionist Quakers,
making himself unpopular among some of them because of
his dramatic protests and outbursts against slavery. He tried
to shame them into fighting more fiercely. He was also a
vegetarian and a defender of animal rights—ahead of his time
in more ways than one.

But right now I want to talk to you of another matter,
something that has been with me for almost three decades. I
want to talk to you about a book. The book itself is a pleasant
read, but the story of what happened to it in reality is not at
all pleasant, and yet now that book and that reality will always
be mentioned together.

You remember the fatwa by Ayatollah Khomeini against
the writer Salman Rushdie? It was issued on February 14,
1989, just over thirty years ago. You might not remember it
as well as I do, because it became one of my obsessions, one
that I have returned to again and again over the years. When
The Satanic Verses was published in 1988, some Muslims
considered the book blasphemous. Living in Iran at the time,
I followed the news surrounding the ensuing fatwa as closely
as I could. You might remember that friends and relatives
who lived abroad, including my brother, Mohammad, tried
to keep us updated on recent events around the world. Even
before the fatwa was issued, the book had sparked widespread
protests among the Muslim communities around the

world, particularly in India and Pakistan. The fatwa further
inflamed these protests. It also led many people, especially
in democratic countries, foremost among them writers, to
oppose the decree as a fatal threat to freedom of expression.

Particularly painful for Rushdie must have been the
many assassination attempts against those who supported
him, among them two Noble Prize winners in literature—
playwright Wole Soyinka of Nigeria and the prolific Egyptian
fiction writer Naguib Mahfouz—both of whom had criticized
Khomeini. Soyinka was threatened with death, and Mahfouz
was stabbed in the neck by an Islamic fundamentalist. William
Nygaard, the Norwegian publisher of *The Satanic Verses*, was
seriously injured after being shot three times. The Turkish
writer Aziz Nesin, who was translating the book into Turkish,
was believed to be the target of arson in a hotel in Sivas,
Turkey, that left thirty-seven people dead. The Japanese
translator of the book was murdered. In Bombay, twelve
protestors died during a riot, and there were book burnings in
Britain. Rushdie himself went underground, with round-the-
clock police protection.

According to Ayatollah Khomeini, Rushdie deserved death
because his book had mocked the Prophet Mohammad and
Islam. I remember one evening, soon after the fatwa, when
some of our friends were at our place, and we had a heated
debate about the issue. You had dropped by to visit the
children but were drawn into our discussion in the living
room. You stood next to the wall, listening, then you said
suddenly, "Your Mr. Rushdie is quite mischievous! Even the
title must sound insulting to our ayatollah." You reminded
us that *Satanic Verses* refers to an unflattering account of the
Prophet that claims when he was confronted and pressured by

the resistance of Mecca's leading merchants to the new faith of Islam, he accepted three of their local deities. I would discover that this account recorded by two Muslim scholars, al-Waqidi (AD 747–823) and al-Tabari (AD 839–923), was discredited by later commentators on the Quran.

Baba, I remember how during those terrible years, you always tried to calm me down. As much as anyone, you hated the Islamic regime and what it was doing to our country and people, yet you would remind me of all the other disasters and tragedies Iran had survived in its two and a half millennia. I wish I had paid more attention when you tried to tell me that we should not be so arrogant as to think our suffering is the only suffering in the history of the world or this country—our country. I knew you were right, but I could not let it go. Had such an edict against a writer been issued anywhere other than my homeland, I would have taken it hard and personally. But the fact that it was delivered by Ayatollah Khomeini, in Iran, made it even harder and more personal.

ALTHOUGH I HAD RETURNED TO Iran from the United States in 1979, after finishing my degree, by the time of the fatwa against Rushdie, ten years later, I still had not adjusted to the Islamic Republic—I never would. After years of being away from my homeland and dreaming about returning there, it was hard to accept that I had come back to a country where such atrocities could occur. As an Iranian and one who was deeply committed to literature and freedom of expression, I felt frustrated and outraged that I could not voice my protest publicly. The new regime's oppressive laws against women and minorities and any form of dissent were accompanied by a systematic assault on freedom of expression and culture. The fatwa confirmed my belief in the close association between imagination and reality: suppression of one inevitably leads to suppression of the other. I had become obsessed with the ideology that shaped Ayatollah Khomeini's mindset, the way that it had penetrated every aspect of our lives. He had taken up all of my mental space, making life itself claustrophobic.

Three decades later, I have the benefit of hindsight. I know that in that moment, in the living room, I did not express myself in a calm and collected way. I blurted out my feelings and emotions, unable to control my outrage. I saw the concern in your eyes. Perhaps you were wondering how I could bear to live in Iran when I almost always seemed to be on the verge of a new outburst.

I am now trying to correct myself by laying out why it was that I acted this way. Baba, I have always felt that the writers and poets in Iran, perhaps more than those in any other country, could truly empathize with what Rushdie was going through, because the same regime that had issued the fatwa against him was the one that censored, jailed, tortured, and even killed us too. Now, close to the thirtieth anniversary of the fatwa, I want to return to it with you. Three decades may have passed, but the issue at the core of the fatwa—the hostility of tyrants to imagination and ideas—is as relevant as ever. And it is relevant not only in dictatorial societies like Iran but in democracies like America as well.

I DON'T THINK YOU EVER actually read *The Satanic Verses*. I first read it in Iran about a year after the fatwa, thanks to my kind and courageous friend in London, Shiva, who smuggled it in on a visit to Tehran. I had a great time reading it, appreciating Rushdie's mischievous play with words, the way he blows them into being like a child blowing soap bubbles, watching them go every which way. I believe the main theme of *The Satanic Verses* was expressed in the book itself by the poet Baal: "What kind of idea are you? Are you the kind that compromises, does deals, accommodates itself to society, aims to find a niche, to survive; or are you the cussed, bloody-minded, ramrod-backed type of damnfool notion that would rather break than sway with the breeze?—the kind that will almost certainly, ninety-nine times out of hundred, be smashed to bits; but, the hundredth time, will change the world."

You, Baba jan, would like this book. It is not about comforting clichés, but ideas that question and disturb and attempt to change the world—which makes not only writing but also reading it so dangerous. And this is what makes such a book so intolerable to tyrannical mindsets. In fact, this is what makes any great work of imagination a threat. Imagination cannot be controlled and regimented; it is free and wayward, refusing to be reduced into any one ideology.

Then there are the phantasmagorical characters living and suffering in the magical realistic world Rushdie has created for them. He must have had a great deal of fun creating the two protagonists in *The Satanic Verses*, who are both Indian actors with Muslim backgrounds: Gibreel Farishta, a Bollywood superstar, and Saladin Chamcha, who has abandoned his Indian identity and is a voice-over actor in England. When we meet the two, their hijacked plane has exploded over the English Channel, and, miraculously, both not only survive but also are transformed. Gibreel becomes the archangel Gabriel, his transformation a symptom of schizophrenia (partly, at least), while Saladin grows hooves and horns, turning into the devil. He is arrested and suffers at the hands of the police, who suspect him to be an illegal immigrant.

I wish you had read the book, because then you would have seen what the ayatollah missed when he condemned Rushdie's novel as anti-Muslim: its objectionable parts are, in fact, the hallucinations and dreams of Gibreel, not Rushdie's own opinions. In Gibreel's dream sequences, a merchant named Mahound—an allusion to Mohammad—appears, and, in a brothel in a city called Jahillia, prostitutes assume the names of the Prophet's wives in order to promote their business. Jahillia, meaning ignorance and stupidity in Arabic, is also attributed to the pre-Islamic era in Arabia, where people were unaware of the grace of God and his Prophet. Now, Baba jan, Rushdie has been accused of blasphemy for his depiction of the Prophet Mohammad, but it is quite clear to any fair-minded reader that it is not him, Salman Rushdie, but his character, the drunken, schizophrenic Gibreel, who sees Mohammad in this light. And never mind that there is really nothing terrible about Mahound except for the fact that he is too human and fallible, and—as some critics have mentioned—a bit like the Christ figure in Martin Scorsese's film *The Last Temptation of Christ*.

Baba jan, I draw your attention to the fact that *The Satanic Verses* portrays a world and a place created by the mind of a madman, where faith, ethics, and knowledge do not exist; where no one is who they claim to be, but all are fabricated versions; a place where character and morality do not matter; where the names of good people are taken to hide the depravity of the rulers; and where the Prophet's wives are degraded in a ploy to make more money. Everything in this world is a parody and an evil shadow of the real world. Rushdie has been quite clear that *The Satanic Verses* is not about Islam but about "migration, metamorphosis, divided selves, love, death, London and Bombay." He claims, "It's a novel which happened to contain a castigation of Western materialism. The tone is comic."

In fact, rather than being critical of Islam or the Prophet, the book is really a critique of not just Western materialism and commercialism but also of clerics such as Ayatollah Khomeini, who seem to claim to have taken up the mantle of the Prophet. In the book, there is a cleric, "a bearded and turbaned Imam," similar to Ayatollah Khomeini, who lives in exile in London, and flies on the back of Gibreel to his homeland when the revolution against the Westernized system breaks out. After all, Rushdie has claimed that "A powerful tribe of clerics has taken over Islam. These are the contemporary Thought Police."

IT IS NOW SOMETIME LATER in the morning. After writing you for a while, I took a break to call my friend in Iran, Shirin, via WhatsApp. You, of course, remember Shirin. You had seen her and talked to her many times, and, once I'd returned to the United States, she told me you were regularly in touch with her. You would ask her to join you at your office for coffee and a chat. This was the third time I'd tried calling Shirin, but to no avail. For the past few days, I have been distracted by an old anxiety: another wave of protests in Iran, accompanied by the regime's ruthless violence.

These protests started over a sudden 50 percent hike in

the price of petroleum. Then they soon became political, calling for the overthrow of the regime and ouster of the supreme leader. What must be particularly frightening for the regime is the fact that people from all walks of life, especially the middle and lower classes, are participating all over Iran. The news, as reported in the media and by human rights organizations, is that the regime has been ruthless, shooting into the crowds from the state-owned buildings, targeting the protestors trying to get away. It has been reported that they have even been shooting from a helicopter. So far, hundreds have been killed, and there are reports of the regime abducting the bodies of the dead and injured in order to hide the real numbers. Families of the victims not only do not know where their loved ones are, but also there are stories about the regime demanding that the families pay for the cost of the bullets or destroyed property—something it has done before to political opponents.

Although I know that the regime has blocked all internet service to Iran in order to stop the news from getting outside of the country, I still keep trying to call my friend, as if I could connect to her through some sort of magic. I am sorry, Baba; every time we talk about Iran, we talk of violence and anguish. For me, of course, there is also guilt, the fact that I live here safe from the bullets, and, despite the anxiety and pain in the back of my mind, I continue with my normal life. All these years, I have been away from Iran, but the feeling of guilt persists almost as if I had just left it.

YOU KNOW, BABA, I HAVE BEEN thinking about what it meant to me that I grew up in a secular, liberal Muslim family. Your version of religion was filled with love and tolerance; a sort of poetic vision. I remember you telling me, as well as writing in your diary addressed to me, about how, at a very young age, you rebelled against the religious fanaticism that was prevalent in some of your relatives—especially an uncle of yours who tried to lead you to the path of righteousness. I still have his letter to you. You had told him you could not believe that of all the billions of people in the world, only the few belonging to your uncle's religious sect would go to heaven. You said that for you, religion was love, and, in response, he accused you of harboring ideas belonging to the "apostate sect," the Sufis! The Sufis now are repressed and victimized by the Islamic regime for believing that individuals can communicate with God directly, without any need for intermediaries. Their shrines have been demolished, their members arrested, tortured, and, in some cases, killed.

I still remember you telling me, in a voice tinged with wonder, that all the prophets performed miracles to prove they were genuine messengers of God, and that Mohammad's miracle was the Word: Quran. It stayed with me, your explanation that at a time when Arabs boasted of the beauty and elegance of their poems, Quran's miracle was that it surpassed them all. Do you remember, Baba, telling me, "And you know, Mohammad was illiterate, God's gift to him was knowledge through poetry?" It has since become painfully clear to me that your version of Islam is not the only one. Ayatollah Khomeini, for one, was there to prove that, like all other religions, Islam has many different interpretations. In case of my home country of Iran, I could not help but feel that religion was a kind of victim, used and

manipulated as a political ideology to maintain the power of
the state.

I WILL NOT SPEND TIME, especially not with you, explaining why
The Satanic Verses is not anti-Islam; the book is its own
justification. I agree with Harold Bloom that it transcends
"political and religious considerations" and that its purpose
"is neither to exalt nor to debase Islam, or its Prophet,
but to tell an enchanting story, and to add strangeness to
beauty." The essential thing is to defend the book's right
to exist, a right that is at the heart of any democracy. I
think you agree that the whole point of fiction is that it is
fiction and should be treated as such. We enter dangerous
territory when we blur the lines between fiction and reality,
or weaponize fiction to further an agenda—be it political,
religious, or personal. The totalitarian mindset breaks the
borders between fiction and reality, and, in the same manner,
it imposes its own fictions and mythologies on the realities
of its people, speaking and acting on their behalf. You see
this mindset not only in authoritarian countries but also in
democracies—the most obvious in America being Trump's
replacing reality with his lies and illusions.

EVER SINCE I HEARD ABOUT the protests and carnage wreaked
by the Islamic regime, I feel invaded by the same emotions I
experienced when living in Tehran. I used to wake up in the
middle of the night, unable to breathe, my heart thumping,
a feeling of claustrophobia, as if I would never ever get out of

the Islamic Republic—*no way out!* Some nights I would have hallucinations, believing I saw an apparition beckoning from a dark corner of the room. I spent many nights awake, rereading my favorite books, especially the mystery novels.

Now, thousands of miles away from Iran, in Washington, the apparitions return, and so do the sleepless nights. There is no getting away from the Islamic Republic. I imagine the victims of the recent protests, mainly young people. My own unforgotten ghosts return: my two younger cousins, sitting on the edge of where we elder siblings and cousins sat, listening to our discussions in fascinated silence. They smiled, mostly, as if they were sharing a secret joke. Or was the smile to hide their intimidation as we talked endlessly with pompous innocence about Jean-Paul Sartre and Albert Camus? How could we know that, a few years later, they of the shy smiles would be arrested for joining a militant opposition organization and executed?

Then there were former comrades from the Iranian student movement in America. They belonged to an opposing, more militant, faction. Soon after the 1979 revolution, they had the illusion that they could lead a people's uprising against the regime. They paid for their idealism with their lives. In America, we'd met almost every day. Yet as I stared at newspaper photographs of their show trials and heard of their torture and eventual executions, I realized how very little we knew about one another personally.

I TOOK A BREAK, attempted another futile call to Shirin in Tehran, then made myself some coffee. I drank it while watching the river from the living room window. Yesterday it rained incessantly, and today the river is a little muddy colored, but still it glows with the welcome sun. It occurs to me that Salman Rushdie was well known amongst Iranian readers before the publication of *The Satanic Verses*. Two of his previous books, *Midnight's Children* and *Shame*, were popular in Iran, and *Shame* was given the state's highest award for best translation. So it was not only writers and intellectuals who were outraged by the fatwa, but also everyday Iranian readers who had so enjoyed his work. I just remembered that, before the fatwa, you had read *Midnight's Children*, wanting to know what all the fuss was about. I told you it reminded me of an absolute favorite novel of mine from the eighteenth century, *Tristram Shandy*, by Laurence Sterne. Both Rushdie and Sterne, I remarked, were mischievous writers. "Yes," you said, "I can see what you mean."

"Well," you added, "a heavy price to pay for mischief."

More than three decades after the fatwa, Rushdie's book is as relevant as ever. In 1989 he said that what he expresses in *The Satanic Verses* is a "discomfort with a plural identity." As he explained: "We are increasingly becoming a world of migrants, made up of bits and fragments from here, there. We are here. And we have never really left anywhere we have been." The migrant experience—bewildering, fragmented, and at times frightening—is one of the main themes of *The Satanic Verses*. In a sense, the book predicted the United States' own anti-immigrant wave, which Donald Trump rode to power.

AT THE TIME THE FATWA was declared, I had just returned to teaching, seven years after my expulsion from the University of Tehran for refusing to wear the mandatory veil. As you well know, before the Islamic Revolution, the universities were not segregated, and women had freedom of choice in terms of their appearance. With the Islamic Republic, all this changed. Like society at large, though, universities went through periods where the rules were relaxed a little, though never for long. When I returned to teaching, the academy was in a more liberal phase, and I chose to teach at the most liberal university in Iran.

I so well remember how happy you were with my decision. I particularly recall you telling me that regimes like the Islamic Republic make us withdraw from the world and other people, and we have to find creative ways to connect. Teaching, you felt, was one of the best ways to do so. When I complained that the officials at the university and the Islamic organizations did not allow me to have an honest and open relationship with my students, you said with such certainty, almost glee, that you were confident I would find a way around the officials. You said, "People like you are far more intelligent and resourceful than they are. You will find a way to hoodwink them." You might not remember this, but I do. You added: "Who knows, it might even be fun." Your smile could be described only as mischievous!

Teaching had always been a joyous and liberating job for me, but after my return, the joy was dampened. Despite the promise of more openness, almost every week I found myself in the office of the dean of Faculty of Literature and Languages, being rebuked for a new offense: not wearing my veil properly, discussing forbidden matters in class, being too informal and intimate with the students, bringing inappropriate speakers to the campus. Under such circumstances, there was no way that I could discuss the "Rushdie affair" in class or in any other public space.

In my diary, in order to avoid the paralyzing effects of frustration and anger, I tried to place the fatwa within some sort of historical context. I ended up tracing it back 2,400 years to Plato's *Republic*, in which, for the first time, the philosopher king exiled the poet. It seems that *The Republic* is the first recorded example of the ongoing war between those in seats of power and those who speak truth to it.

I first read *The Republic* during my junior year at the University of Oklahoma. Baba jan, I just have to tell you this: almost every time I tell someone here that I went to the University of Oklahoma, they say, "How on earth did you find Oklahoma? An Iranian girl studying English literature at the University of Oklahoma?!" I tell them I got married to someone who went to that university. I was the only foreigner in the Department of English, and I thoroughly enjoyed my classes. And, by the way, I also discovered the beauty of fireflies and red earth. Many are surprised when I tell them how liberal OU was at the time, with its students participating in all sorts of protests, including the antiwar movement. We even took over the administration building!

Anyway, I first read Plato in a seminar with Professor James Yoch called "Backgrounds to Renaissance." Remember Professor Yoch? You and Mother met him when you visited me in Norman, Oklahoma. From the very start, I felt exasperated by *The Republic*, although I now confess that my reaction was a bit extreme. What bothered me most was Socrates's edict that the Homeric poet, being a mere "imitator thrice removed," has no place in his ideal republic. How could any republic survive, I asked, without the two human faculties that work through imagination: curiosity and empathy? Not only would literature and the arts cease to exist without imagination, but science would as well. I found it ironic that despite Plato's severe edict against poets, he himself was a great literary stylist with a talent for brilliant metaphor.

Professor Yoch was amused by my reaction, and most of my classmates couldn't figure out what all the fuss was about—except for one, Dan. He too felt that Plato's *Republic* was fuss worthy, but he believed that I was gravely mistaken in my unruly and passionate objections to it. If there was anything Dan could not bear, it was unruliness; order was his motto. Everything about Dan was impeccable—from the buttoned-up corduroy shirts he wore, to the careful cut of his hair. We spent hours together over coffee discussing Plato; our disagreements over *The Republic* had created a certain bond between us, preserved mainly by his calm demeanor and the fact that he never responded in kind to my heated and angry arguments. Dan adored Plato. If there was any writer that he loved and revered more, it was the novelist Ayn Rand, whose superior characters Dan felt were essential to the health and well-being of a nation. (*Health* was his favorite word when applied to the ideal society.)

One night I stayed up late poring over Socrates's discussion of the "noble lie" in *The Republic*. Plato is after a "well-ordered state," with the philosopher king at the top. You will remember that in order to preserve the state, Socrates suggests the noble lie, which should be told to the laymen as a kind of "medicine" to help ordinary citizens stay in their place and facilitate the rule of the philosophers. According to this lie, the republic is composed of a hierarchy. At the top are the guardians/philosophers, whose souls God has mixed with gold and who are "competent to govern." Next come the auxiliaries, or warriors, whose souls contain silver. And at the bottom are the farmers and craftsmen, whose souls are mixed with iron and bronze.

Baba jan, suddenly I saw why Socrates's state was so hostile toward poets and storytellers. Within such a hierarchy, there was no place for poets who indulge in "irrational nature," which is the "inferior part of the soul." They were not utilitarian, could not rule, or make people more virtuous. Even worse, their tales might "engender" the "laxity of morals among the young." According to Plato, the Homeric kind of poets bring confusion and "The greater the poetical charm of them, the less are they meet for the ears of boys and men who are meant to be free and who should fear slavery more than death." Sound familiar?

To me, Plato's arguments against the poet were laughable, and I arrived at our seminar the next day prepared with my counterarguments. Dan kept quiet in class but afterward invited me for coffee at Ernie's Diner, a popular campus hangout. We sat opposite each other in the orange leather booth, and, over coffee and donuts, Dan explained his views on the noble lie, how I was misunderstanding its complex nature, and how it was necessary for reining in the unruly populace. Dan liked Socrates's idea of the well-ordered state, and felt that it was right for the republic to be based on a hierarchy headed by the philosopher king.

I disagreed, insisting that Socrates's division of the citizenry into three categories based on the noble lie was totally bogus. To begin with, the term "the noble lie" implies that it was not true, and it was also elitist in the worst sense of the word.

Dan began lecturing me on why ordinary people needed the guidance and wisdom of superior beings, without whom society would be ruled by chaos. He continued to explain that there was the bad kind of lie, and then there was the noble lie told by the wise philosophers. That lie, as I would know if I had read my Plato properly, was like medicine to society and its citizens—it was for their own good. Every government, he would say, even the democratic ones, were all based on some sort of mythology, some version of the noble lie. There was something disturbing about Dan's calm justification of the noble lie and his quotations from Ayn Rand's novels. Equally as disturbing, I was becoming consumed by *The Republic* and by Ayn Rand, whose characters, although I laughed at them, both repulsed and obsessed me.

I could not have imagined then, as I drank countless cups of coffee at Ernie's, arguing earnestly with Dan, that just a few years later, after obtaining my PhD, I would return to Iran just as the Islamic Revolution was beginning. Indeed, I would end up living in a modern theocratic version of Plato's *Republic*. Returning to Plato in the Islamic Republic, I thought of Dan and his reproach and realized that I had not really appreciated the complexity of Plato's ideas. Today, as I think back to our friendly debates, I recognize that Socrates's arguments made me question and think and reevaluate even while I opposed them. I have also come to recognize how exceptional it was that Dan and I, despite our deep differences, managed to have so many thought-provoking arguments with such tolerance and appreciation for the other's view. But I still disagree with his ideas on Plato, and my objections to Socrates's treatment of the poet remain as strong as ever.

Perhaps the philosopher king and the poet were always destined to be at odds. Baba jan, I have little doubt about this, having seen the proof of it in both the Islamic Republic and America. These seem to be two opposing worldviews, with one trying to control and maintain power at all costs, and the other constantly questioning and attempting to subvert that power. As soon as you leave the well-ordered hierarchical and static state of the republic, you enter the noisy, overcrowded, chaotic, and (there's that word again) mischievous world of the poet, where complexities interfere and contradictions abound. In the poet's world, heroes are flawed, and everything is tinged with doubt and ambiguity. "Go for broke," Rushdie, the poet, advises us, adding, "Always try and do too much. Dispense with safety nets. Take a deep breath before you begin talking. Aim for the stars. Keep grinning. Be bloody-minded. Argue with the world. And never forget that writing is as close as we get to keeping a hold on the thousand and one things— childhood, certainties, cities, doubts, dreams, instants, phrases, parents, loves—that go on slipping, like sand, through our fingers." The noble lie is a safety net; a way of keeping us in line. Rushdie the poet would tell us to dispense with it, to be "bloody-minded." What choice does the king have but to kick the poets and storytellers out of his republic? And what choice does the poet have but to destabilize the philosopher king's power by speaking the truth?

Dear Baba, we don't know if Ayatollah Khomeini ever read Plato. We can safely say that Donald Trump never did, and no one would ever call him a philosopher king or accuse him of deep philosophical thinking. But both Trump and Khomeini follow the same patterns, bring the same arguments, and act

in the same manner. And we also know that Salman Rushdie
is guilty of the same offenses as the poet who was so long ago
exiled from the republic.

Whatever we call this figure, whether "philosopher king,"
"supreme leader," "führer," "father of the nation," or "Mr.
President," we are talking about the same thing. It has long
been in the nature of poets, thinkers, artists, musicians,
writers, scientists, journalists to resist power; freedom of
expression for them is in their blood, running through
their veins. Rushdie himself has asked, "What is freedom of
expression?" adding, "Without the freedom to offend, it ceases
to exist." In *The Satanic Verses*, he proclaims, "A poet's work is
to name the unnamable, to point at frauds, to take sides, start
arguments, shape the world, and stop it from going to sleep."
One side creates the noble lie to preserve order and power; the
other side attempts, through art, to replace the lie with the
disturbing and subversive truth.

IT IS LATE AFTERNOON. I took a break from writing you, trying
to call Iran. Apparently, the internet is back but not in all
places. As usual, every few hours, I check the news about Iran.
Several hundred have been killed and thousands arrested,
abducted from their homes and workplaces, without their
families knowing where they are or what has happened to
them. Khamenei, the supreme leader, is reported to have said,
"Do whatever it takes!" to end the protests.

I tried calling Shirin on WhatsApp several times without
success. Then I received a voicemail from her, saying that the
internet had just returned, and the lines were probably very
busy. In a sarcastic tone, she said not to worry, that all was

secure and under control. "And I mean *under control*," she repeated with a small laugh. I keep drinking coffee and dialing Tehran—I need something more calming than coffee. How do you deal, Baba, with a system whose response to any form of opposition is elimination? How do you deal with it, when they are the ones holding the guns and have no hesitation in using them? At times like this, I feel I am out of sync with America, where few seem to care about what goes on in other parts of the world. Over here, it is so difficult for many to accept that such atrocities happen, and that they can happen here as well. If we treat the prisoners in Abu Ghraib or Guantanamo so brutally, we are capable of doing the same to our "domestic enemies."

Rushdie seems to have dealt with his predicament by continuing to write and thereby gaining some control over his life. For a while, they took away his freedom of movement, forcing his life underground, but they could not suppress his voice, his words.

AND NOW HERE I AM in the United States of America, near the end of the year 2019, again thinking of Plato, his Socrates, and the philosopher king quarreling with the poet. To my great dismay, since the 2016 elections, I have been having many of the same kinds of reactions to the news and to Trump that I had in Iran regarding the Ayatollah Khomeini. I find myself talking back to Trump and his enablers on the television, getting worked up, leaving the room, and even writing him scathing letters.

I know, I know: Trump is not Ayatollah Khomeini, and America is not Iran. Trump shares with Khomeini,

however, a specific mindset, an attitude. I can see the
same trends, the same traits working here. My hope lies
in the fact that America is still a democratic society with
democratic institutions that can stand up to Trump and his
administration.

You and I have not forgotten the fierce and unrelenting
enthusiasm with which so many Iranians welcomed Ayatollah
Khomeini back to Iran in 1979, after fifteen years of exile
had been forced upon him because of his attempts to foment
uprisings against Shah Mohammad Reza Pahlavi. How could
we forget? His return coincided with the overthrow of the
shah and ended the country's 2,500 years of monarchy. You
were right when you claimed that many among Khomeini's
supporters had no idea who this man really was or what he
had in mind for Iran. They were blinded by their demand
that the old system must go, without having any idea what
they wanted to replace it with. Don't you think that there is
a moment in most political upheavals when people lose their
individual voices and become one, when a sort of blindness
takes over their faculties, and that is the decisive moment that
can allow a tyrannical mindset to take over?

We used to talk a lot about such issues, trying to make
sense of how and why this revolution succeeded. It wasn't just
that, from its inception, the Islamic regime used violence and
fear to quash opposition. It was also the fact that so many,
especially those among the political and intellectual elite,
either supported the regime or remained silent. You and I
were stunned that so many chose to ignore the ominous signs:
the murders and executions, the mistreatment of women and
minorities, the replacement of progressive laws with regressive
and brutal ones. When the new regime executed the old

government officials— or innocent people accused falsely of collaborating with that government—many remained silent, and the majority of political organizations and groups, both inside and outside Iran, including some on the Left, supported the Islamic regime's actions. One by one, opposition groups and individuals, dissidents who defended human rights, women who poured out into the streets asking for their confiscated rights, and minorities both ethnic and religious, were silenced, jailed, tortured, and killed. Eventually the regime began to punish its own members, and the jails filled with defectors who had once ardently supported Ayatollah Khomeini.

These questions, dear Baba, always remain: What if we had not given in to the frenzy? What if we had not remained silent and complicit? There are lessons here for those who live in democratic societies, who fail to see the creeping, insidious signs threatening an open society. "How could such a thing happen in Iran?" they ask innocently. One could respond by asking, "How could Trump happen in America?" We must not be blind to what has been happening in so many democratic societies, including the United States.

Trump's rise to power in America was in some ways similar to Khomeini's rise in Iran. Trump saw an opportunity. Meanwhile, a large number of people were deeply unhappy with the state of the country, and they lacked confidence in the political establishment. He understood how to captivate the media, and to use their obsession with him to his advantage. He entertained us with his buffoonery, and this blinded us to what was really happening, and what had been happening for years: the corporate mentality, the utilitarianism and focus on money, the neglect of civic responsibilities, the cynicism and lack of trust, all leading to the current state of affairs. Khomeini, you might say, was no buffoon, and, of course, you would be right, but he similarly mesmerized people with his talk of God and spirituality.

DEAR BABA, YOU DID NOT have access to my writings after I left Iran for America. You only heard about them from friends or from my interviews with Voice of America and the BBC. So you perhaps don't know that for the past few years, I have been writing and speaking about the ways that totalitarian traits appear not only in totalitarian societies but in democracies as well. These appearances may seem sudden and unexpected, but, in fact, they are rooted in weaknesses that have been there all along. It is at times like this that we realize once more the centrality of imagination and ideas to the health and well-being of a democratic society. This is why I keep returning to Rushdie's work and to his conflict with the ayatollah. We need the poet to constantly question things as they are, to jolt us out of our comfort zones, to make us look at the world through the eyes of others and seek to understand experiences that are not our own. As opposed to the lies we hear from Trump and his cohorts, we need the truth that fiction offers us. But over here, many are either indifferent to imagination and ideas or demand that art and literature follow their own conception of reality.

These are some of the reasons to return again to Plato's *Republic*—specifically to a section that Dan and I overlooked. I am talking about the famous allegory of the cave, a beautiful example of the extended metaphor in *The Republic*. Don't you find it ironic that Plato, who threw the poet out of his republic, should use his literary talents so well to convince his readers and to prove his points?

Baba, I am not sure how much of *The Republic* you remember. The allegory of the cave is narrated by Socrates at the beginning of book seven. Socrates tells Glaucon, Plato's older brother and his interlocutor, about a people who "live under the earth in a cave-like dwelling." They have been shackled by the neck and legs and cannot move, not even to turn their heads. The only thing these prisoners are able to see is the blank wall of the cave in front of them. Behind and above the cave, at some distance, a fire is burning, and between the people inside the cave and the fire is a walkway, in front of which hangs a curtain wall, like a puppeteer's screen.

People pass by the walkway, carrying "statues and other carvings made of stone or wood" behind the curtain wall. The brightness of the fire behind the curtain projects the objects' shadows onto the back wall of the cave where the prisoners can see them. These shadows comprise the prisoners' only reality. Otherwise they have no idea of the outside world. They are used to this world and even content to live there. So far, we have an allegory of a people living in the darkness of ignorance; a world populated by shadows.

Now imagine this: one of the inmates somehow breaks free of his chains, leaves the cave, and sees the fire outside. But he is not happy; the light from the fire hurts his eyes. In such a case, Socrates asks Glaucon, would not this person, his eyes burning with the glare of the fire, prefer to return to that cave? After the darkness of ignorance, the glare of enlightenment is painful. However, the inmate undergoes a torturous and difficult process, first getting used to the light from the fire and then, later, even looking at the sunlight that is the source of all lights and shadows. It will take time before his eyes can get used to the sun and therefore the truth. So, he goes back to the cave, where he tries to convince his fellow prisoners to see the reality behind the shadows. But the others are angry with him and think of him as dangerous. They want to be comfortable in the shadow of their ignorance and are afraid of being blinded by the light of the truth. Socrates asks Glaucon, "And if they can get hold of this person who takes it in hand to free them from their chains and to lead them up, and if they could kill him, will they not actually kill him?" To which Glaucon responds, "They certainly will."

There is an inherent contradiction between Plato's search for truth and his advocacy of the noble lie. When I read *The Republic* today, one of things that I take away from it is that it is not true that we all want the freedom of knowledge, because it comes at a high price. It comes with pain and loneliness; it demands commitment and responsibility.

The most seductive aspect of a totalitarian society is the security it offers. The truth is uncomfortable, and a dictator promises an abdication of responsibility from it. In America, I think it's safe to say that most of Trump's supporters are with him not because they respect Trump, or think that he is an honorable man, or are impressed with his vast knowledge of foreign policy. Instead, they feel secure in his promise to run the country like a business (financial comfort) and are consoled by the idea that he will "Make America Great Again" (spiritual comfort).

THIS AFTERNOON, AS I TOOK a break for coffee, I dialed Tehran once more and finally connected to Shirin. Now that I had

her on the phone, I felt tongue-tied. I could only ask her
repeatedly if she and her family were all right. She sounded
ironic and bitter, telling me how "safe" and "sound" they
were—so safe, she added, that they couldn't even leave home
to buy bread. Not the regime's fault if people place themselves
in the line of fire; they are asking for it, she said in a mock-
serious tone. What was that young woman Golnar Samsami
doing there in the street waiting for a cab? she asked. Is it the
shooter's fault if she is standing where she could be shot so
easily? And then that thirteen-year-old boy—children these
days, they are so careless, almost asking for it.

If we are not killed by their bullets, she said, we will soon
die of this pollution; schools are closed because of it, and
people mainly stay at home. After a pause, she added, one way
or another, through violence, incompetence, or corruption,
they're going to kill us. While pretending to laugh, the old
feelings of guilt and sorrow returned: I was safe, and my
friends—for the time being—had survived. But then what
about that young woman, and the thirteen-year-old boy, and
all those others who had not been this lucky?

PLATO'S TWO-THOUSAND-YEAR-OLD WARNING about the necessity
of truth, and the difficulty of seeing it, has echoed throughout
literature ever since. Baba, I don't think you have read Ray
Bradbury's dystopian novel *Fahrenheit 451*, first published in
1953 and back on the bestseller lists today. In *Fahrenheit 451*,
in a future American society where books are outlawed and
"firemen" burn any that are found, the inmates of Plato's cave
appear in a different guise. The majority of the characters
in Bradbury's classic are not chained physically. Still, they

perceive only what is planned for them; they choose to live in a shadow world, not the real one.

In democratic societies, we do not normally resort to physical violence to muffle those with ideas, but we do use other forms of violence: prejudice, censorship, and slander. Totalitarianism comes with an inflexible ideology that divides the world into two opposing camps: the good and the bad. "If you don't want a man unhappy politically," says Beatty, the fire chief in *Fahrenheit 451*, "don't give him two sides to a question to worry him, give him one. Better yet, give him none." In this manner, we are saved from the doubts, complications, and contradictions we might face through making individual choices and accepting responsibility for them. Like the prisoners in Plato's cave, we need not tolerate the glare of the sun.

Baba jan, I now empathize with the fact that although you were political all your life, you avoided all political ideologies. Ideology always needs an invented enemy to keep supporters excited and on their toes and to keep rebels frightened and paralyzed. As we in Iran discovered so painfully, it is easy to invent enemies when you see the world in black and white. In *Fahrenheit 451*, the most dangerous objects are books. Books know no limits or borders, they create new longings and unexpected passions, they pose more questions than answers. They represent the unruly world, filled with contradictions and complications, a world that threatens the totalitarian mindset by being beyond its control.

In the world of *Fahrenheit 451*, anyone who refuses to turn over their contraband books is considered a lunatic and a rebel, and the government has created a mechanical dog to sniff out

the rebels and destroy them. Like the prisoner who leaves
Plato's cave, a firefighter named Guy Montag, whose job is
to burn the possessions of those who read books, is gradually
and painfully enlightened. His first initiation into the world
outside his cave is through meeting a young neighbor, Clarisse
McClellan ("seventeen and insane," she tells him). Through
their few meetings, Clarisse gradually opens Montag's eyes to
the possibility of a different world. She reacquaints him with
his forgotten senses: the taste of the rain, for example, and the
colors of grass and flowers. Montag had forgotten to see, to
hear, to taste, to touch, and to feel the world.

"I sometimes think drivers don't know what grass is, or
flowers, because they never see them slowly," Clarisse tells
him. "If you showed a driver a green blur, Oh yes! he'd say,
that's grass! A pink blur! That's a rose garden." She alerts the
fireman to the violence that has been forced upon them, the
disregard for being human and for human life. Clarisse tells
Montag that at school, she is called antisocial by those who
never ask questions. She says she is afraid of "children my own
age. They kill each other. . . . Six of my friends have been shot
in the last year alone. Ten of them died in car wrecks." Not
long afterward, Clarisse is struck and killed by some of those
"children" who apparently run over people for the fun of it.

I can't help but think of another kind of violence now so
prevalent in America: the mass shootings, turning places such
as schools, churches, shopping centers, places where we felt
safe, into such dangerous and unsafe spaces. Our son, Dara,
was on the campus at Virginia Tech during the mass shooting
there in 2007. I remember how that morning, in between
trying to connect to Dara's cell phone and listening to the

news, I kept thinking that my husband and I had managed to keep our children safe through a war and a revolution in Iran, but not safe here in a small town in America.

Montag tells his wife, Mildred, "We need not to be let alone," adding, "We need to be really bothered once in a while. How long is it since you were *really* bothered? About something important, about something real?" This, Baba jan, is a question everyone in America should ask themselves. Montag begins to ask questions, then steals books and tries to educate his wife and her friends. Finally, after authorities have ordered that his house be torched, he kills the fire chief and goes on the run, eventually escaping to the countryside to join a community of exiled book lovers.

Totalitarianism is often associated with extreme pain and violence. And the world of *Fahrenheit 451* is not exempt from this. Fear and uncertainty are always present. This is a place where neighbors, friends, and family spy on and report one another. But no system can rule by fear alone. Authoritarians also employ another, more subtle, method: they seduce us with intellectual and spiritual comfort.

Dear Baba, time and again I go back to our discussions about how fear and seduction work hand in hand. I return to Rushdie's quote about the poet: "A poet's work is to name the unnamable, to point at frauds, to take sides, start arguments, shape the world, and stop it going to sleep." In *Fahrenheit 451*, the state thinks for the citizens and rewards them for not thinking. They abdicate responsibility and cannot be punished for their actions, which have been predetermined. When we stop thinking, we stop caring. And, as Bradbury says, we "bombard people with sensation" that "substitutes for thinking." Once we allow ourselves to be seduced, we give up our free will. Beatty, the fire chief in *Fahrenheit 451*, says, "Remember, the firemen are barely necessary. The public itself stopped reading of its own accord." Dearest Baba, I am so reminded of life in today's America.

Before his escape, Montag lives in a luxurious shadow world. Instead of being lined with books, Montag's and Mildred's living room has three walls covered from top to bottom with huge television sets that provide "parlor games" for viewers to participate in. Mildred, like the majority of residents of her city, is addicted to these games and to her television "family," looking forward to the day when they have enough money to cover the fourth wall with TVs. Baba jan, you have not lived in America today to know how descriptive this is of everyday life in this country. It is not only censorship that is dangerous to the well-being of a society but also the mindlessness created by the constant demand for entertainment and sensationalism; a desire to remain on the surface and avoid the complexities and difficulties presented by ideas and imagination.

Just to show you how prescient Bradbury was, right before his book was published in 1953, he said, "In writing the short novel *Fahrenheit 451*, I thought I was describing a world that might evolve in four or five decades. But only a few weeks ago, in Beverly Hills one night, a husband and wife passed me, walking their dog. I stood staring after them, absolutely stunned. The woman held in one hand a small cigarette-package-sized radio, its antenna quivering. From this sprang tiny copper wires which ended in a dainty cone plugged into her right ear. There she was, oblivious to man and dog, listening to far winds and whispers and soap-opera cries, sleep-walking, helped up and down curbs by a husband who might just as well not have been there. This was *not* fiction."

Now, Baba jan, almost seven decades after the book's initial publication, the devices Bradbury was so worried about have become part and parcel of our lives: we walk down the streets, eat in restaurants, and meet with friends, glued to our iPhones, unaware of the life around and about us. Was Bradbury predicting a future where our devices would become expansions of not just our bodies but also our minds? You and I have had no discussions on virtual reality, which became so pervasive after your death. The way I see it, virtual reality, the internet, are beneficial as long as they enhance our lives. They become dangerous, though, when they replace reality; when we evade what is real in pursuit of the virtual.

We don't need a supreme leader to deprive us of our hard-earned freedoms. When we stop reading, we pave the way toward book burning; when we stop caring, we make way for someone else to take over control; when we prefer personality to character, and reality show or virtual reality to reality itself, then we get the kind of politicians that we deserve.

Dear Baba, my worry is that this polarization, along with more and more dependance on virtual reality, prevents us from connecting with other human beings and with the real world. This lack of connection dehumanizes not just others but also ourselves.

YOU MIGHT WANT TO KNOW how this story ends and whether there will be any hope for a society such as the one Bradbury portrays. In his community of exiled book lovers, surrounded by sounds and smells of nature, Montag hears the ominous sound of jets moving across the skies, omens of the looming nuclear war that will soon destroy the city and most of its inhabitants. The rebels seem to be preparing for the future, when a world destroyed by war and totalitarian rule will be rebuilt. In order to do this, each of them has memorized a book, so that even if all the books are destroyed physically, they will remain. Oblivion is an accomplice to death, and books have always been guardians of our memory. Now human beings will become guardians of books. "Reading," Ray Bradbury said in an interview, "is at the center of our lives. The library is our brain. Without the library, you have no civilization."

DEAREST BABA, IT HAS BEEN three decades since the fatwa. I still believe that tyrants may go but tyranny remains unless we find the right way to fight it. It is easy to become the carbon copy of the tyrant, to talk and act like him, dehumanizing your adversary, but this is what Rushdie avoids, despite all the violence committed against him. The rebels in *Fahrenheit 451* avoid this temptation as well. They are focused on one thing that you were focused on: self-examination and self-criticism. One of them, known only as Granger, tells Montag, "We all made the *right* kind of mistakes, or we wouldn't be here. When we were separate individuals, all we had was rage." While outrage is rightly our first reaction to cruelty and corruption, we have to transcend this reaction. "The most important single thing we had to pound into ourselves," Granger says, "is that we were not important, we mustn't be pendants; we were not to feel superior to anyone else in the world." Instead, he insists that their job is to remember, to resurrect the books, and that they must reflect on and criticize themselves rather than obsessing on those they escaped from. "Come on now," Granger tells Montag, "we're going to go build a mirror factory first and put out nothing but mirrors for the next year and take a long look in them." These lines are so close, Baba, to your way of thinking. I really wish you had read *Fahrenheit 451*.

BABA JAN, ONE MORE THING before I end this letter: talking of the confrontation between the philosopher king and the poet, I was reminded of something that had struck me while living in the Islamic Republic. You remember that after the revolution, the Islamic regime took down the statues of the shah and his father and changed the names of streets and squares that bore their names. The regime also wanted to bring down the statue of our great epic poet, Ferdowsi, who had written of Iran's ancient pre-Islamic glories and kings, and also change the name of the street named after the agnostic poet and astrologer Omar Khayyam. But people's love of these poets forced the authorities to back down. Not only that, but, decades after the revolution, the regime had to acknowledge defeat and celebrate the same poet whose statue it had tried to bring down.

Khomeini could bring down the king but not the poet. In the words of Shakespeare:

Not marble nor gilded monuments
Of princes, shall outlive this powerful rhyme.

I am sure you agree that Ferdowsi neither believed in the benevolence of the world, nor of the kings; he believed in his poetry, ending the *Shahnameh* with these words:

I've reached the end of this great history
And all land will fill with talk of me:
I shall not die, these seeds I've sown will save
My name and reputation from the grave,
And men of sense and wisdom will proclaim,
When I have gone, my praises and my fame.

With love,
Baba's daughter,
Azi

HURSTON, MORRISON

Dearest Baba,

It was difficult getting out of bed this morning, although I was awake by five. I turned on the light and started rereading passages from Zora Neale Hurston's autobiography, *Dust Tracks on a Road*. But I couldn't focus. I felt light-headed and anxious, almost on the verge of a panic attack. I got up, treating myself gently, as if I were holding my own hand, like an invalid, and walked myself to the kitchen, where I made some coffee. On the dining room table lay a few enlarged photographs of protestors killed in the November protests in Iran that I mentioned in my previous letter. They were all young and looked unbearably alive, these strangers now made intimate, finding their way into my dining room because of their deaths.

The photos were out for a candlelight vigil that Bijan and I attended last night, commemorating the fortieth day of mourning for those killed. It is difficult to pinpoint the number of the dead. Amnesty International has confirmed at least 304 people; Reuters reports 1,500. We will never know the real numbers; the regime has warned families of the victims against so much as talking to the media. Perhaps the feeling I woke up with was the remnant of last night's experience. A small crowd of us had gathered on Dupont Circle in DC. With us was Ladan, my cousin Abdi's wife; for the past two decades, the two of them have been our close and intimate friends. You most probably knew Ladan's father, Abdorrahman Boroumand, who was a close associate of Shapour Bakhtiar, the last prime minister under the shah. He, like Bakhtiar, was knifed to death in front of his Paris apartment by the Islamic regime's agents in 1991. Ladan and her sister, Roya, founded a human rights center in their father's name. Time and again, Ladan and Roya have repeated that the reason for their organization was justice— not revenge.

It was a mild night for the end of December, one of those days when the sky is the color of winter and the temperature that of early fall, creating a sense of confusion, this discrepancy between how it looks and how it feels. I kept thinking how different this vigil was from the protests and vigils we held in Iran, where every moment was tinged with fear of attacks by the regime and its vigilantes. This vigil was peaceful and calm. The fear at the back of my mind was merely a remnant from my experiences in Iran.

Later, Bijan, Ladan, and I went to a favorite restaurant, where Abdi was waiting for us. But I couldn't get rid of this feeling of hopelessness, of defeat, of so many killed, thousands injured, arrested, or disappeared. How many times over the past forty years have people poured into the streets in protest against the regime? Each time, the protests grow in number, the slogans become more radical, yet each time the regime quashes them with unbelievable violence. What was the point?

Dear Baba, I called Shirin to talk about this, and we both agreed that for as long as this regime is in power, people will protest, the government will try to kill them, and we abroad will hold vigils and demonstrate. She said these protests have become important less because there is hope of changing the regime but more just to remind the ayatollahs: we are here, and we will resist you. And to remind ourselves to not give in to the conditions they have created for us.

At six o'clock, I turned on *Morning Joe*, which is what we do every morning, but today I was not really listening. Anyway, the news in Trump's America makes me even more jittery, more irritated, and frustrated. For a long time now, I have been increasingly anxious about the direction this country has been moving toward. I have written about it, talked about it, and now simply feel exhausted by it. Every time I talk about Iran, usually someone would come up with concern and sympathy in their voice, asking what he or she can do for "them," talking as if dictatorships and totalitarianism can happen only elsewhere—there but not here. It *can* happen here. Perhaps it is already happening.

AS AN ANTIDOTE TO MY feelings of frustration and despair, I want to talk to you about Zora Neale Hurston and her novel *Their Eyes Were Watching God*. She is quite a woman! The best way to describe her is in her own words: "No, I don't weep at the world. I am too busy sharpening my oyster knife." I have always found this statement empowering; I love its tone of defiance. As an African American woman with high intellectual ambitions in the first half of the twentieth century, Hurston had every reason to "weep at the world," but she did not. A woman after your own heart, Baba jan, some might call her foolhardy, but I call her feisty and spirited. Her empowered defiance is just what we need in these trying times.

If I remember correctly, many, in fact, called *you* foolhardy, or spirited, depending on who said it. The way you write in your memoirs, it seems you have always been stubborn, a rebel, a contrarian. I think of how, in your sophomore year in high school, you led a boycott and protest against a teacher who had been unfair in his grading, all the way to the local office of the Ministry of Education and Culture. I so vividly remember your accounts of how, as a young man, you left your family and city for Tehran, choosing a wife and a lifestyle your father disapproved of—and then, of course, you preferred jail and an uncertain future to freedom and all the bonuses that came with it. You told us these stories about yourself and others, and I imagined them. They became a part of me, as if I had been physically present at the events you so colorfully created for us.

I am reminded of your journalist friend Mr. Safipur, who once told me, "You have a pair of stubborn parents, each stubborn in their own way. Your father appears to be the flexible one, but, then, he spent four years in jail, refusing to write a letter of contrition, which would have earned him not just a pardon but a juicy job and a return to the fold."

MY GOD, BABA JAN, decades have passed since you were kept at the temporary detention center for four years on trumped-up charges without a trial, but for me, it is literally as if it were

yesterday. I don't need to go back to those days, because a
part of me is always back there. I was only a teenager then,
but I had to act grown up and pretend I was not affected by
what had happened to you. I put up a brave front. The truth,
which I never told you, was that I was scared and shocked.
One moment you were the youngest and most popular mayor
of Tehran: you spent time with the president of France, who
gave you the Légion d'Honneur; with the king and queen of
Denmark; the chancellor of Germany; the presidents of the
Soviet Union and India; and the vice president of the United
States. The next moment, you were in jail.

Our house after your arrest was a meeting place for friends
and well-wishers. They gathered there every Friday morning,
drinking mother's Turkish coffee while discussing your fate
and exchanging news and gossip. One Friday morning, as I
sat vacant eyed, listening to the cacophony of voices, your old
friend the wonderful Mr. Khalighi, who always reminded me
of a kind and gentle crow, took pity on me, took me aside, and
tried to answer some of my questions. I couldn't understand:
If my father was not guilty of what they arrested him for, then
why did they arrest him?

Mr. Khalighi tried to explain why you were both innocent
and in jail. He said you were paying for your "mulishness."
"Your father," he said, "has a lot of good qualities, but is not
made for politics; he is too mulish." He told me that from
the very start, when you became mayor, you had problems
with the prime minister and the minister of the interior.
What seemed to be a matter of independence to you felt
like pigheaded arrogance to them. Things came to a boil,
Mr. Khalighi told me, over the uprising of June 5 and 6,
1963, when thousands of people came into the streets to

protest Ayatollah Khomeini's arrest because he'd denounced the shah's progressive reforms, especially the one about enfranchisement of women.

According to Mr. Khalighi, the prime minister told you the day before the protests that they would be taking a hard line, and that you, as mayor, should instruct the shops to close down, tell the hospitals to refuse treatment to protesters, and, under no circumstances, have any contacts with the clerics. "Your father," Mr. Khalighi said, "disobeyed all three orders; in fact, he even had the shops open earlier than usual so that people could do their shopping before the streets were filled with the demonstrators and the police.

"That," he said, shaking his head, "sealed his fate. A few months later, they arrested him."

According to your friend, your enemies wanted you to learn your lesson, express regret, and ask for forgiveness, "But," he said, "your father is too mulish, he says he wants to clear his name and will stay in jail until a trial where he will publicly answer their charges and defend his reputation." Later, I understood this mulishness, when the head of the secret service paid you a friendly visit in jail, letting you know that if you merely wrote a letter of contrition, you would be set free. Instead, you wrote a letter responding to every single charge brought against you and refused to leave jail until you had your trial and your say. To friends and family, you explained, "I have to save my name; that's all I have." You did so.

But eventually, according to Mr. Safipur, keeping you in jail was costing your adversaries more than letting you have your trial. Your story appeared not only in Iranian media but also beyond the country's borders, including in an article in the *Washington Post*. You can imagine how we felt when finally, after four years, you did get to defend yourself at a closed trial. We were not allowed to be present, but later we knew that you offered your own defense, refuting all charges. What an exhilarating moment it was when we heard you were exonerated of them all except for insubordination, something we were very proud of. I was almost sorry when, later, they also dropped that charge—insubordination within the context of your arrest was more a badge of honor than of shame.

I was and still am proud of you, but after those four years, I lost my trust in anyone in power—I became a true anti-establishmentarian. Your time in jail also cost me my sense of stability and security; never again did I feel at home in my own home. But at every stage in my life, even when I belonged to a political organization, at critical junctures I have been reminded of the importance of being mulish when it comes to one's sense of dignity.

REREADING AMERICAN FICTION AFTER MY return to America, I found myself fascinated by the way that American authors have created fictional heroes and heroines out of the most marginalized members of society. One of the many great contributions of African American writers to American culture is the variety of new fictional characters they have introduced to readers, thus expanding the horizons of both reality and fiction: Ralph Ellison's invisible man, James Baldwin's Rufus Scott and John Grimes, Zora Neale Hurston's Janie Crawford, Richard Wright's Bigger Thomas, Toni Morrison's Pecola Breedlove, and so many others.

I want to talk to you about two of these characters: Pecola Breedlove from Morrison's *The Bluest Eye*, and Hurston's Janie

Crawford in *Their Eyes Were Watching God*. They are both a reaction to a condition imposed on African Americans, one that James Baldwin describes very well. In a 1970 letter to Angela Davis, Baldwin claims, "The American triumph in which the American tragedy has always been implicit— was to make black people despise themselves." The question becomes: How do we react when an outside force tries to take away our sense of self and turn us into a figment of their imagination? Both *The Bluest Eye* and *Their Eyes Were Watching God* are, on one level, a reaction to this sense of self-contempt imposed upon not just African Americans but also any oppressed people.

Which is how I came to think of the protagonists in *The Bluest Eye* and *Their Eyes Were Watching God*. Pecola Breedlove and Janie Crawford, both African American women oppressed because of their race and gender, are two very different individuals—near opposites, in fact. One is a victim who has no chance against the system, and the other is an independent woman who doesn't even acknowledge the system.

I will begin with Toni Morrison and Pecola Breedlove. Morrison died just a few months ago, and for me, talking about her work with you is a way of both mourning her death and celebrating her life.

I REMEMBER SO WELL WHEN I first read *The Bluest Eye*. It was during one of my trips in the nineties to the United States. You remember that between the winter of 1989–90 and 1997, when I migrated to the US for good, I would travel there for speaking engagements and conferences. I don't need to remind you that not long after I returned to Iran in 1979, my passport was taken—ironically, because of my antigovernment activities during the shah's time—and I could not leave the country for another eleven years. This was an emotional time for me, during which I began to believe that I would never be able to leave Iran, never mind return to America. You must remember how I kept bugging you about my predicament and how you prescribed patience, reminding me in vain that things will never stay the same.

I have not talked to you much about my experiences during those trips, the sense of excitement and of freedom, alongside the guilt of being unable to share this with my family. Each time I visited America, I found myself in thrall to the smallest personal freedoms, such as seeing a film uncensored in a real cinema, or walking down the street without the mandatory veil that hid my hair in Iran, or hearing sirens and knowing immediately that it was just an ambulance and not a warning that my city was to be bombed.

During each visit, in between meetings and talks, what I looked forward to most was visiting the bookstores. This sudden access to books that I never could have gotten my hands on in Iran made me feel like the proverbial kid in a candy store. Once, after a talk at the University of Pennsylvania, I left one bookstore with, if I remember correctly, Sylvia Plath's *Ariel*, Muriel Spark's *Loitering with Intent* (which became my favorite of all her books), Heinrich Boll's *The Clown*, and Toni Morrison's *The Bluest Eye*. I had read Morrison's *Beloved* in Iran, courtesy of a friend who lived in the States, and was curious to know more about her work.

The Bluest Eye, which I soon began referring to as "Pecola" after its anguished protagonist, is a short novel, and I read most of it during my flight back to Tehran. It is the story of a young African American girl, Pecola Breedlove, growing up in America during the Great Depression. Pecola believes that she is hideously ugly and develops a destructive dream: to have blue eyes like the white women she holds as the standard for beauty. I empathized immediately with Pecola.

Dear Baba, I know that during the time you were at the American University in Washington, DC, on a grant, you thought often about racism in America. I came across one diary of yours from then in which you wrote of "that sorry state of affairs" in a country like America that boasts so much about freedom and equality. So you would understand how the systemic effects of racism in America make Pecola feel deeply ashamed of who she is and the way she looks. Total power demands total subjugation, without which it cannot rule. In Pecola's case, even her body is transgressive. The young girl feels ugly and worthless because she is a Black woman, one who doesn't live up to society's standards of beauty. On top of that, she is raped by her own father and has no way to defend herself. What she is denied is her autonomy, her individuality, and her right to choose. She has no way of knowing and owning up to who she really is. She defines herself by who she is not: namely, a blue-eyed white woman. For someone like Pecola, who so depended on the way she looked, there is no such thing as "self-revelation."

YOU MUST REMEMBER MY TRIPS to America, if for no reason other than the stress they put you under. I was so used to turning to you whenever I had a problem, as if simply revealing my fears and anxieties to you would cause them to magically disappear. Each visit, you would share with me both excitement and anxiety. I am grateful to you for listening to my premonitions about how I would be stopped in the airport and prevented from leaving, how they would once more confiscate my passport, how I would never make it. All through this, you would sit there with an indulgent smile. Once, you told me, "I think they have more urgent worries than you to think about." Then more seriously, you said, "Anything might happen, but if you have made the decision to take the risk and go on these trips, then try to relax and enjoy yourself; plenty of time to worry in case things go wrong." And yet you were worried enough to accompany me to the airport from the first time I left Iran to the last.

Before I left Tehran for that conference in America in the winter of 1989, and each time after that when I traveled abroad, Iran's Ministry of Higher Education summoned me for a threatening lecture before issuing permission for my travels. I was told that while abroad I was still to act according to the laws of the Islamic Republic, refrain from criticizing the regime, and dress as modestly as I did in Iran. However, I did not follow these orders. After each trip I took, on my way home, I would be overwhelmed by fear of being found out, of being punished. And yet each time I left Iran for an international conference, I would do the same thing. You can empathize, Baba jan, the truth being that obeying the regime's orders diminished me, made me feel ashamed of myself, as if an alien had taken over my body.

I INHERITED FROM YOU THE terrible habit of underlining my books and writing in the margins. I remember how, in your youth, you wrote your travel diaries in the margins of poetry by the

fourteenth-century Persian poet known as Hāfez. My notes
scrawled throughout that copy of *The Bluest Eye* were not
about my own fears and anguish. They were about Morrison's
protagonist, a victim trapped by the lies and illusions spun
to keep her in her place. This is the central struggle between
those in power and the storytellers: the fight over the meaning
of truth, the tension between illusion and imagination.
Imagination reveals the truth, clarifies it, while illusion hides
the truth, turning it opaque. I will repeat Baldwin one more
time: "The American triumph in which the American tragedy
has always been implicit—was to make black people despise
themselves."

We read and write stories for many reasons, including
to take revenge on society's injustices. Morrison's novel,
published in 1970, is one such story of revenge. Could you
believe that it had been banned from libraries and schools for
its depiction of incest, rape, racism, and child molestation?
Pecola has not only been raped by her father, resulting in
pregnancy and a stillborn child, she is also the victim of the
daily acts of malice and cruelty inflicted upon her because
of the color of her skin. She is vilified for being "ugly" and
learns to see and define herself through others' definition of
her. Equating beauty with whiteness, she becomes a victim
of lies presented to her as absolute truths. "It occurred to
Pecola some time ago that if her eyes, those eyes that held
the pictures, and knew the sights—if those eyes of hers were
different, that is to say beautiful—she herself would be
different." She fervently and hopelessly wishes for blue eyes,
believing that once she has them, she will be beautiful and
loved. Her obsessive urge to become that all-powerful white

"other" by acquiring a pair of blue eyes deprives Pecola of ever knowing her own beauty. "Thrown in this way, into the binding conviction that only a miracle could relieve her, she would never know her beauty," Morrison writes. "She would see only what there was to see: the eyes of other people."

In the end, Pecola becomes insane, believing that somehow her wish has been granted and that her eyes have turned blue. She then worries that someone else might have bluer, more beautiful eyes than she has. The only ones to empathize with her are the novel's narrator, Claudia Macteer—Pecola's foster sister for a short while—and Claudia's own sister, Frieda. Claudia summarizes their community's treatment of Pecola this way: "All of our waste which we dumped on her and which she absorbed. All of our beauty, beauty, which was hers first and which she gave to us."

MORRISON USES POETRY TO EXPRESS Pecola's inner beauty, one that is hidden from the world and from Pecola herself. *The Bluest Eye* has even been called a poem. The book's poetry lies in the author's revelation of the inner beauty of her characters, even as they live lives of humiliation and poverty. What humiliates them most, white supremacy, is itself a lie. By creating a poetic language for her characters, even those who commit unspeakable acts, she negates the claims of the racist masters that have been absorbed as belief by the oppressed Blacks. This is Morrison's way of demanding justice for Pecola and her race—by bringing out their true beauty, far more lasting than a pair of blue eyes.

Baba jan, I believe that through Pecola's story and the

poetic beauty Morrison bestows on it, the novel not only avenges the injustices against African Americans, but against all victims of prejudice and hatred. While Pecola's story itself is tragic, Morrison restores dignity to her protagonist by exposing the lies and mythologies that Pecola's oppressors use to keep her enslaved. By telling Pecola's story, Morrison returns her life's ownership to her, revealing the truth. In Morrison's words from *Beloved*: "Freeing yourself was one thing; claiming ownership of that freed self was another." I believe you would appreciate such sentiment.

I REMEMBER HOW, DURING YOUR time in jail, you constantly used poetry to explain yourself to friends and foe. I was so touched by your poems to my brother Mohammad and me in which you reminded us that our father was not a criminal—as you said, the criminals are free, roaming the streets. You wrote poems to our mother, to Aunt Nafiseh, to Uncle Reza and his wife, Ashraf—in each one, explaining your feelings about them. But you also wrote poems to the shah, the minister of justice, and to your interrogator, telling how you felt about what was being done to you. You write in your memoirs with some glee that they neither liked nor understood poetry, which somehow gave you the upper hand. I remember that at your trial in your last defense, you began with a poem by our epic poet Ferdowsi and mentioned additional poets, Persian and otherwise, throughout your argument. You were writing and reading dangerously. Poetry was a way to combat the staid and formulaic language of politicians that opposed the flexible and dynamic language of poets and writers.

I was impressed by the way you had hit upon a unique

means of resistance. They wanted you in jail in order to break you, and you resisted by choosing an attitude and language that was foreign to them, showing them you were not broken.

REREADING PECOLA'S STORY REMINDED ME of *Their Eyes Were Watching God*, although, or perhaps because, Morrison's protagonist and Hurston's are very different from each other. What interests me is how each reacts to her dual oppression as an African American and as a woman.

The work of Zora Neale Hurston was introduced to me in the mid-1970s by a feminist activist. It's ironic that Hurston, who refused to be defined by any sort of -ism, later became such an icon of feminism. Although I don't remember this activist's name or the circumstances under which we met, I have a distinct memory of her short blonde hair and very pale blue eyes. I was drawn to her because she was so adamantly a feminist, and I was so adamantly not a feminist—I instead considered myself a Marxist. Yet deep down, I was curious about feminism. At the time, I was active in the Confederation of Iranian Students, composed of anti-shah Iranian students and political groups. Our membership was based mainly in Europe and the United States. I was drawn to the leftist politics in vogue in the sixties and seventies. But I was also ambivalent toward the political and ideological movements. I'd always had my quarrels with the movement, never feeling completely at home, but when it came to politics, I towed the line for a short while. And one aspect of that line shunned any form of individualism, calling feminism too bourgeois, an attitude that put women's rights ahead of the more universal anti-imperialist, anti-capitalist struggle. Isn't it ironic that I, who believed I was fighting for my country's liberation and independence, had abdicated my own independence for the sake of a political ideology?

I remember that during one of our debates about feminism, this woman who had recommended Hurston looked at me with what seemed like pity. That look has stayed with me. It was far more effective in converting me to her cause than any argument she put forward in defense of the primacy of women's rights. Without being willing to admit it, I must have empathized with her anyway.

This feminist activist recommended that I read Alice Walker's 1975 *Ms.* magazine piece "In Search of Zora Neale Hurston," and I savored Walker's adventures as she searched for Zora's grave in a dilapidated all-Black cemetery called the Garden of the Heavenly Rest, in Fort Pierce, Florida, being bitten by bugs and trying to avoid the snakes. After reading the piece, I was eager to read this elusive and funky lady named Zora Neale Hurston myself. But her book was not reissued in the United States until 1978, and by then, I was too focused on the events at home that led to the Islamic Revolution. It would be two more decades before I read *Their Eyes Were Watching God*.

Her novel's protagonist, Janie Mae Crawford, is a biracial woman in search of love and fulfilment. Disappointed by her first two marriages, she defies convention by falling in love with and marrying Vergible "Tea Cake" Woods, a poor man twelve years younger than she is. Janie is after love rather than security in marriage, and her sense of self is very different from Pecola's. Hurston's focus in the novel seems to be more on Janie's inner life and her relations with the three men in her life than on an overt condemnation of race and racial politics.

When I finally read *Their Eyes Were Watching God*, I liked it so much that I considered including it in a course I had thought of teaching about the subversive roles of women in fiction. In my research for the course, I identified Janie Crawford as the descendent of a long line of female fictional protagonists in eighteenth- and nineteenth-century English and American literature, which includes Samuel Richardson's Clarissa Harlowe, Jane Austen's Elizabeth Bennet, Charlotte Brontë's Jane Eyre, Henry James's Daisy Miller, and Kate Chopin's Edna Pontellier. These women all defied the customs and mores of their times, risked a great deal—at times their lives—in order to follow the dictates of their own hearts. Their decisions are personal but have political, social, and cultural reverberations that go to the heart of freedom of choice.

HURSTON WAS CASTIGATED BY SOME of her prominent male African American peers, who accused her of kowtowing to the white race by ignoring racial politics. Alain Locke, the prestigious and eminent critic and scholar of Black literature during the 1920s through his death in 1954, wanted her to "come to grips with" the kind of writing he called "motive fiction" and "social document fiction." Richard Wright, whose *Native Son* became a blockbuster bestseller in 1940, was particularly hard on her, claiming that *Their Eyes Were Watching God* "carries no theme, no message, no thought."

Baba jan, you must be smiling! Perhaps you are reminded

of the heated debates between the writers and intellectuals in Iran over commitment to literature, over the question of whether literature is a vehicle for political messaging or, rather, an independent entity. Hurston's approach to literature and politics was quite different from that of many of her critics. Later, she criticized Wright's *Uncle Tom's Children*, published in 1938, accusing it of being dominated by hatred. This harsh review was not merely her responding in kind to Wright's broadside against her own work. I say this because I believe that in essence the quarrel between Hurston and Wright was one between two opposing attitudes toward fiction. Wright, at that time, saw fiction mainly as a vehicle for political ideology, whereas Hurston avoided political agendas and ideologies and focused on the individual. In my view, that focus makes Hurston a better storyteller. But, of course, American fiction needs both Bigger Thomas and Janie Mae Crawford.

Dear Baba, Hurston believed that storytelling was an individual act, focused on individuals through whom the story connects to multitudes. I believe that fiction, as she saw it, was about the dignity of the individual. Therefore the task of fiction was not to issue manifestos or messages but to place readers within individual experiences, making them understand and empathize through that unique experience. Preserving individual dignity was central to both Hurston's life and her work. Wright, on the other hand, was interested in social realism, or the protest novel, wherein individuals were subservient to social and political causes. At the time, Wright's was the dominant attitude. In *Native Son*, Bigger Thomas is a victim of racism and oppression. Everything he does, including the crimes he commits, is rooted in that. He accidentally kills the white daughter of his employer, but then murders his own girlfriend, fearing that she might report his crime. It is only in jail, when he is at death's door, that he understands the consequences of his actions. Bigger is always a victim of his circumstances; unlike Janie, he never develops or grows enough to denounce his victimhood and take responsibility for his actions. Hurston's protagonist, in contrast, never accepts or succumbs to being a victim.

There is this 1997 essay on Hurston by Claudia Roth Pierpont in the *New Yorker* titled "A Society of One, Zora Neale Hurston, American Contrarian." Pierpont argues that although Wright's novel became an immediate blockbuster, there was nothing new about the kind of protagonist he presented in Bigger Thomas. Southern literature had offered similar characters for a long time. What changed with Bigger was "the author's color and the blame." Pierpont reminds us of the irony that while Wright's novel went on to become a Book-of-the-Month Club bestseller despite its biting critique of America and its ideological claims, Hurston's book, which made no such claims, was panned by prestigious Black authors for shying away from social and political matters. *Their Eyes Were Watching God* went out of print, and Hurston nearly starved. Meanwhile, both the African American intellectual elite and white critics and readers welcomed Wright's book. "For the first time in America," Pierpont writes, "a substantial white audience preferred to be shot at."

I believe Hurston's view of fiction was more revolutionary, as it transcended politics and defied a sense of victimization to emphasize individual dignity. Janie Crawford, like her creator, is her own woman, and, like her creator, refuses to be defined by anyone but herself. Her strong sense of dignity compels her to refute any form of authority in her life.

Dear Baba, there are two things I'd like to note in appreciation of Hurston's work: first, she writes about Blacks without the domineering shadow of whites constantly hovering above them; and, second, she writes about the lives of individuals rather than Black representatives of a race, thereby rescuing her characters from generalizations and labels and turning them into individuals. Is it because Hurston was raised in Eatonville, Florida, an all-Black town ruled solely by Black people, that she so focused on her people and their inner lives rather than on overt racism? By that, I don't mean to say that she was not conscious of racism and its devastating effects on the lives of African Americans. In a passage in her autobiography that was deleted by her publisher, Hurston criticizes Western colonialism and racism in America, linking slavery to other forms of oppression: "I just think it would be a good thing for the Anglo-Saxon to get the idea out of his head that everybody else owes him something just for being blonde." She goes on to say, "The idea of human slavery is so deeply grounded that the pink-toes can't get it out of their system. It has just been decided to move the slave quarters further away from the house."

You, Baba jan, with your sensitivity against racism, would have appreciated Hurston. Instead of presenting a generalized portrait of African Americans as victims, I believe she wanted to rescue them from stereotypes imposed on them and restore the individual dignity and humanity that slavery and racism had stolen from them. This is one reason Janie cannot be categorized. She does not fulfil our expectations of what a "Negro woman" should be—and she certainly defies the mores and expectations of her society. It would take feminist readers decades after the initial publication of *Their Eyes Are*

Watching God to discover Janie. When it comes to reflecting the experience of life as a Black woman, she is every bit as real as Pecola.

One of Hurston's essays, "You Don't Know Us Negroes," is scathingly critical of how whites perceive African Americans. In this piece, she talks about how slavery had persuaded most whites to look at African Americans as "creatures of task alone." But, she goes on to explain, "in fact, the conflict between what we wanted to do and what we were forced to do intensified our inner life instead of destroying it." Hurston concludes by saying that "Negro reality is a hundred times more imaginative and entertaining than anything that has ever been hatched up over a typewriter."

Despite her criticism of white people in this essay, her focus as a novelist was on Black characters and their relationships. As I see it, she wanted African Americans to unburden themselves of white domination, reprimanding the "intellectual lynching that Black people perpetrated upon themselves whenever they sought to emulate whites, in art or in life." She tells her Black readers: "Roll your eyes in ecstasy and ape his every move, but until we have placed something upon his street corner that is our own, we are right back where we were when they filed our iron collar off." Her exquisite novel is her subversive way of placing "something" on that street corner that is her own.

BABA JAN, I WANT TO talk to you about the events in Iran. I have become obsessive. I constantly check the news on Iran, I call my friends back in Tehran just to hear their voices, I look at the photographs of the dead protestors. How much fear must the government feel when its security forces attack the cemeteries around the country to prevent the victims' families and friends from mourning them on the fortieth day of their death?

Shirin said that, in a strange way, this is some form of consolation: they are so afraid of us that they need to kill us in order to feel a bit more secure. But the more they kill, the more people protest. "Of course," Shirin continued, "it shows how desperate people like us have become to believe that being killed is a sort of consolation!" She paused, then added that there seems to be no end in sight.

BABA JAN, LIVING UNDER THE totalitarianism of the Islamic Republic made me appreciate Hurston's viewpoint regarding individual resistance to a corrupt and oppressive system. If you remember, while I was still in Iran, I had come to believe that we were wrong to judge everything by ideological yardsticks, rejecting every point of view that was different from ours. Over time, I, along with some other activists, became disenchanted with some political organizations and groups that claimed to have revolutionary goals and yet sided with Ayatollah Khomeini on many issues—especially that of women's rights, with some even chastising women for their "untimely" protests against the Islamic regime. I was no longer affiliated with any political group or organization, but, at the same time, I could not help but resist the system as a teacher, writer, woman, and believer in human rights.

I did not like the possibility of being arrested, humiliated, and flogged. I did not like the prospect of being expelled from my job or having my books censored and banned. But there

was something greater than fear—or more magnetic than
fear—that was driving me: an instinct for self-preservation.
I knew that giving in to them meant self-negation. It meant
a public abdication of who I was. It had nothing to do with
being an intellectual or sophisticated. It was a matter of self-
worth and what Hurston called "self-revelation" and, of course,
a matter of preserving dignity. Needless to say, I had you as a
model when it came to preserving individual dignity. Let us
just say I started believing in the virtue of being "mulish"!

Political movements are important, but they do not negate
individual resistance. In fact, they complement one another
when the movements are flexible and open. This was one
other topic Shirin and I kept returning to in our conversations.
We talked about how, at the beginning of the revolution, not
many paid attention to women's demands for their rights,
but as time went by, this changed, and now one can say
that women are at the forefront of the struggle against the
Islamic regime and its reactionary laws. However, Iranian
women practiced a different kind of resistance, one that is
not "political" in its narrow sense. These Iranian women,
who came from very different backgrounds and held many
different beliefs, remind me of Hurston, with her desire for
autonomy, her unique form of subversion, and her resilience
expressed so beautifully when she writes, "I have been in
Sorrow's kitchen and licked out all the pots. Then I have stood
on the peaky mountain wrapped in rainbows, with a harp and
a sword in my hands."

I was reminded of this recently while reading the prominent
Iranian writer Shahrnush Parsipur's prison memoir, *Kissing
the Sword*. Shirin reminded me of her and asked me if I had
read her book, and so I did. You remember her, Baba jan? She

was jailed the first time for unspecified charges and remained there for more than four years. For her too, dignity came first. In one section, Parsipur talks about how, on one occasion, her fellow prisoners joined in the noon prayers—regardless of their religious beliefs—but not her. "I strongly believed that I could never pray out of fear or praise God in a manner determined by the Hezbollah," she writes, adding, "I believed that if I did, I would lose my creativity to write. I believed, as I still do, that one of the secrets to being a writer is honesty with oneself." She goes on to say, "A writer might be a coward or an egotist, but if she is mired in dishonesty, the brilliance of her pen and the brightness of her mind will grow dark."

No matter how many times I hear of such cruelty and suffering, I still can't get used to it; I still react as if I am hearing it for the first time. Parsipur witnessed unimaginable brutalities in jail. One night, she and her cell mates had stayed up listening for single bullet shots delivered to the head, as a way of tallying the number of prisoners executed. That night, they counted more than 250. Parsipur herself had been placed in solitary confinement. She had seen the tortured bodies of those who had disobeyed, and yet there was something in her that made her resist because she was a writer. Her desire to write, as well as her belief in democracy under any circumstances, were her main sources of sustenance in the years she spent in jail despite no charges against her. In deciding not to pray, Parsipur had defied not only her jailers but also her fellow victims, her cell mates. "I had seen," she writes, "how quickly people changed from tortures and executions and the constant emotional pressures." She had concluded that if she allowed herself "to bend under pressure," and pray like other prisoners, she would make it possible for them to bend her even more. She adds that "my belief in democracy made me want to preserve myself as I was and to make it clear to the others that I was not one of them. And so, with great trepidation and with the knowledge that my decision could worsen my circumstances, I decided not to pray."

I first met Parsipur at a meeting of Iran's Writers Association, where she read her short story "Fa'izeh," in which a prostitute begins to see all men as headless. After her reading, some writers among the audience accused her of having no political ideology, her story having no political message in tow. Yet her stories were indeed more subversive than the more blatantly political stories written by her accusers. She was later jailed three times in the Islamic Republic, one of those times because of her book *Women Without Men*, which focused only on women. "Fa'izeh," which appeared in that book, had apparently offended the regime with its portrayal of a prostitute as worthy of dignity and understanding. Not surprising, considering that under the Islamic Republic's laws, prostitution is punishable by stoning to death.

Some years after Parsipur's reading at the Writers Association, by which time she'd been released from jail, I, along with a few other writers, visited her at her home. In a calm, objective tone, she told us stories of the brutality and torture she had suffered. After we left, I was still recovering from the experience of hearing her stories when one of the writers said, "Intellectual women, when they are young, attract attention through their looks, and, when older, they do so through becoming political!" I told him sarcastically that it wasn't only the Islamic regime that needed an education in women's liberation and walked off. And I meant it, Baba jan. Here was a prominent writer, an opponent of the regime, who, nevertheless, had the same mentality as the regime when it came to women. And he was not the only one to think like that; I had come across quite number of a people who should have known better. Parsipur was very independent, she belonged to no political organizations or groups and had no political ideology, and she paid a heavy price for being so much herself.

For me, Baba jan, Parsipur's case is an extreme example of what Iranian citizens in general, and Iranian women in particular, have had to suffer. This suffering created a form of resistance that transcended the political forms of struggle. It became personal, much like Janie Crawford's.

I LIVED WITH PECOLA'S ANGUISH until the day I encountered Janie. Many attempts have been made by critics, activists, and feminists to categorize both Janie and her creator, to no satisfactory results. They are both far too complex, contradictory, and alive to allow such a thing. You might ask what is it that makes Hurston subversive. It is the fact that she evades expectations, defies categorizations, provokes questions, and leaves the reader questioning. I know that she claimed to be a Republican and was criticized for neglecting to write fiction in defense of her race in a social documentary fashion, and yet I keep discovering that she wrote some of the most scathing critiques of white people penned by anyone. In fact, I really believe the only constant about her was her independence. As she told her friend Countee Cullen, "I mean to live and die by my own mind." In her autobiography,

Hurston writes, "But I am so put together that I do not have much of a herd instinct. Or if I must be connected with the flock, let *me* be the shepherd of my own self. That is just the way I am made."

Baba jan, I particularly love one story from Hurston's autobiography. As a child, she used to climb to the top of one of the chinaberry trees that guarded their front door and from there "look out over the world." The most interesting thing she saw was the horizon: "Every way I turned, it was there, and the same distance away." One day, when she was nine years old, she decided to walk to the horizon. She asked a friend to accompany her. That friend agreed at first, but when the time came, she reneged on her word, afraid of not getting back home on time and being punished. The walk was canceled, but the magic of the horizon remained. It is this desire for the horizon—her unquenchable passion for something out of reach and yet so close to the heart—that Hurston gives to Janie.

"The eagerness, the burning within," she writes about herself in a letter to her friend and mentor Annie Nathan Meyer, an antisuffragist, promoter of women's higher education, and founder of Barnard College. "I wonder the actual sparks do not fly so that they be seen by all men. Prometheus on his rock, with his liver being consumed as fast as he grows another, is nothing to my dreams." She continues, "I dream such wonderfully complete ones, so radiant in astral beauty." Janie also wants to go to the horizon, and, in fact, in the end, she claims she has been there and back. Janie's dreams, her consuming passions, are what differentiate her from the rest of her community. She tells her friend Pheoby Watson, "Ah been a delegate to de big 'ssociation of life. Yessuh! De Grand Lodge, de big convention of livin' is just

where Ah been dis year and a half y'all ain't seen me." All
I can say is wow!! How can we bear such intensity? Yet life
without it has little meaning or purpose.

DEAR BABA, YOU MIGHT WONDER what role if any does race play
in Hurston's novel. While the plot of *Their Eyes Are Watching
God* focuses on Janie's relationship with the men in her life,
race is an underlying theme. It appears in the relationship
between Janie and her grandmother Nanny rather than
through her direct confrontation with the white race. White
people appear only twice in the story. The first time is after
a terrible storm, when Tea Cake is forced at gunpoint to join
a small army of Black men searching for dead bodies and
burying them. He and the other men have to separate the
white bodies from the Black, because the whites will get
coffins, but the Blacks will just be dumped in a hole. As Tea
Cake tells his fellow grave digger, "They's mighty particular
how dese dead folks goes tuh judgment," adding, "Look lak
dey think God don't know nothin' 'bout de Jim Crow law."
This scene is short but horrendous at the same time, bringing
out the brutality and inhumanity of race relations in America:
Blacks get no rest from whites, be it in life or death.

The second instance is when Janie, on trial for killing Tea
Cake, faces an all-white jury, judge, and defense lawyer, as
well as some sympathetic white women in the audience. This
time her white observers are so taken by her story that she
is acquitted and applauded by the white spectators in the
courtroom gallery. This demonstrates some empathy and
understanding on the part of the whites, as well as credit to

Janie's powers as a storyteller, mesmerizing the crowd. But we must remember that had she killed a white man, even in self-defense, no doubt the situation would have been different. Baba jan, I think you, having gone through a trial yourself, understand why truth matters so much to Janie and why she is so adamant that her story be believed: to deny her story is to deny her, Janie Crawford.

It is more in Janie's relationship with Nanny, and in her deeper family history, that we see race as central to her story. Janie's main quarrel is not with the men in her life but with a certain kind of attitude, a certain mindset that is the result of slavery and racism, which her grandmother exemplifies. At some point in her story after the death of Jody Stark, her second husband, Janie realizes that "she hated her grandmother and had hidden it from herself all these years under a cloak of pity." Janie had been "getting ready for her great journey to the horizons in search of *people*." But "she had been whipped like a cur dog and run off down a back road after *things*." Janie believes everything depends on how you see things. Some people look "at a mud puddle and see an ocean with ships." But her Nanny "had taken the biggest thing God ever made, the horizon," and then had gone on and "pinched it into such a little bit of a thing that she could tie it about her granddaughter's neck tight enough to choke her. She hated the old woman who had twisted her so in the name of love."

The difference between Janie and Nanny, as well as Janie and Pecola, is that Janie "had found a jewel inside herself and she wanted to walk where people could see her and gleam it around," while her grandmother defined herself only in relation to the white masters. She tells Janie, "Honey, de white man is de ruler of everything as fur as Ah been able tuh find out." The plot in the story moves forward through Janie's journey of "self-revelation" and her fight against her grandmother's slave mentality.

Baba jan, we as readers do not agree with Nanny, but we understand her fears and empathize with her. How could we know her life and suffering and *not* empathize with her? Janie's grandmother had been enslaved. She was raped and molested by her white master and beaten and threatened by his wife when she found out about their relations. Nanny had run away and struggled to survive with her little girl in tow, and that girl, Janie's mother, was raped at seventeen and soon disappeared from their lives. Nanny's fears and suffering shape her every move and threaten Janie's dream of the horizon. Through her experiences, Janie gains more independence not only as a woman but also as a person. She has to fight both misogyny and the slave mentality, and, in the end, she achieves a measure of success in both pursuits. Her dream of finding the horizon has been fulfilled. As she tells her friend Phoeby, "Ah done been tuh de horizon and back and now Ah kin set heah in mah house and live by comparisons."

Ultimately, what remains is the power of reclaiming one's freedom and identity through story. When Janie is on trial, she feels she is not fighting death in the courthouse but that she is fighting "lying thoughts." What she wants most is for people to believe the love story between herself and Tea Cake. She fears "misunderstanding," not death. If found guilty, the verdict would mean that she didn't love Tea Cake and wanted him dead. And that would be "a real sin and a shame. It was worse than murder." Janie, found not guilty, is saved by telling her story.

Baba jan, it is true that we all die, but the story remains, enduring long after we are gone. Toni Morrison gets justice for Pecola by telling her story, revealing her inner beauty, the poetry of her being. Hurston tells Janie's story by giving her voice to reveal it herself and to assign her trusted friend Phoeby to tell it to others. This is, as the feminist Persian poet Forough Farrokhzad said, how someone dies and someone endures. This is how we resist the cruelty of man, the fickleness of life, and the absoluteness of death. This is how fiction subverts the absolutist mindset: by defending the right of every individual to exercise their independence of mind and of heart. This is how Janie lives, this is how Hurston lived, and this is how I believe you lived.

With love
Baba's daughter,
Azi

GROSSMAN, ACKERMAN, KHOURY

APRIL 5–MAY 12, 2020

Baba jan, the next writer I want to talk to you about, David Grossman, I have met twice. The first time was in Barcelona, where we were both part of a literary conversation series. The second time was at an event in Washington, DC, a conversation between the two of us, moderated by the then literary editor of *The New Republic*, Leon Wieseltier, on March 20, 2016. I remember the date because it was the evening before the Persian new year.

On both occasions, I found myself unable to summon the words to tell Grossman about the effect his 2008 novel *To the End of the Land* has had on me. The book's story line is both simple and enigmatic: Ora is an Israeli woman whose younger son, Ofer, has gone to war, and she believes that if she is absent when the news should arrive that Ofer has been killed in battle, she can somehow magically avert Ofer's death. It had been a long time since I have felt this way about a work of fiction. Remember how once you described to me how you felt after reading Flaubert's *Madame Bovary*? My feelings while reading *To the End of the Land* were akin to yours regarding Flaubert's novel. I reacted to the book the way I usually react to a poem: feeling it and experiencing it before grasping the meaning or finding words to express it.

But even if I had found the words, what would have been the point of sharing them with Grossman? It was like falling in love with someone and then trying to explain to his parents how much you love their son. Grossman's book, once published, was his, and yet it was also an entity entirely separate from him. I knew that if I tried to express my feelings about it to him, I would become awkward and feel silly and inconsequential. Still, because of some vague and persistent urge, I needed to talk about it with someone. Perhaps, in a roundabout way, I can express to you why I reacted the way I did to *The End of the Land*.

The conversation with Grossman in DC was focused on the capacity of fiction and imaginative language to stand up to those in power. He made two very important points that have stayed with me over the years. The first: "If we can imagine, we are still free." And the second: he mentioned how touched he was when an Egyptian critic reviewed him, an Israeli writer, in the newspaper *Al-Hayat*. If I remember correctly, he said this was the first time his work had been acknowledged in the Arab press, and it was that acknowledgement—the confirmation that he lived not as an anonymous Israeli enemy but as a writer, an individual—that mattered so much to him. That kind of acknowledgement, I believe, is at the core of so much of his writing, in particular, *To the End of the Land*. In his 2007 essay, "Writing in the Dark," Grossman tells us, "I write. I purge myself of one of the dubious but typical talents that arise in a state of war—the talent for being an enemy, nothing but an enemy."

After our conversation, a young man who had been in the

audience approached me to say that he was bewildered by
our focus on imagination at the expense of facts. Facts, he
felt, were central, were real, while imagination was a luxury,
mainly of writers and artists, irrelevant to our everyday lives.
Our real lives. I began to argue that Grossman and I were both
living proof that while facts are important, they do not negate
imagination. My experience of coming from an oppressed
society where the regime considered writers, poets, and artists
as its enemies—where so many of them had been jailed,
tortured, and even killed—was confirmation of how pivotal
imagination is to freedom. Unfortunately for me (and perhaps
fortunately for that young man), I was interrupted by family
and friends who were waiting for me to go.

Baba jan, hope you don't mind if, in deference to that young
man, I will begin with facts rather than fiction. On August 12,
2006, while Grossman was at work on *To the End of the Land*,
his younger son, Uri, an Israeli tank commander, was killed
by a missile that destroyed his tank while he was trying to
rescue soldiers from another tank. This tragedy occurred just
two days before the UN called a cease-fire to end the Second
Lebanon War. And, two days before Uri's death, Grossman,
along with some other prominent writers, had publicly called
for an end to the war. Grossman had started work on *To the
End of the Land* three years before, and he has said that during
his writing, "I had the feeling—or, rather, a wish—that the
book I was writing would protect him." After his son's death,
Grossman returned to writing the book. He mentions, "Most
of it was already written. What changed, above all, was the
echo of the reality in which the final draft was written."

Dear Baba, you might ask, "What about the facts of our
political reality? Do they not have a place in Grossman's

novel?" Immediate political reality interferes in our consideration of his novel; that cannot be helped. But exactly *how* it interferes matters. Grossman is an Israeli writer who has been a political activist and a progressive force in the Arab-Israeli conflict and wars. He is also a vocal critic of the Israeli government's policies regarding the occupation of Palestine and its treatment of Palestinians. He has said that the Israeli people might feel that Israel is their "fortress" but "still not truly their *home*." I also know that while he empathizes with the Palestinian people, he is a critic of their side's leadership too, and that his political positions are based on his principles and not on partisan or ideological agendas and biases.

Having said all of that, facts are not the main reason I read *To the End of the Land*. What intrigues me is that Grossman's books are the offspring of the Israeli-Palestinian conflict, and yet they are not. They protest, but not just in a political sense—they are, in fact, declarations of independence against the brutalities of war and against the brutalities of life itself. His fiction targets existential issues as well as political issues.

Baba jan, I can almost hear you say, "But the fictional facts that create Grossman's novel are as important as the real facts." And you would be right, for in fiction, as in reality, we need to experience the "facts"—in this case, through our imagination—in order to understand them:

Ora is an Israeli physiotherapist in her late forties whose son Ofer has volunteered for a military operation even though he had just fulfilled his military service. In order to do so, he cancels the camping trip to Galilee that he and his mother had planned. In a fit of desperation, Ora forces Avram, her friend, former lover, and Ofer's biological father, to go camping and walk through the land with her. Avram, a soldier during the 1973 Yom Kippur War, had been captured and tortured by the Egyptians, an ordeal that made him withdraw from life and all that he had loved and cherished before.

Ora, Avram, and her now-estranged husband, Ilan, had been intimate friends since their teenage years, having first become close while in the isolation ward of a hospital in Tel Aviv during the Six-Day War of 1967. In the present, Ora, worried that her son may not survive, clings to the belief that as long as she is not home when the military notifiers come, Ofer will remain alive. Ora is *A Woman Fleeing from Bad News*, as the literal translation of the book's Hebrew title indicates. And in fleeing, she uses the magical power of stories to keep her son alive.

In one passage, Grossman casually drops the name of Scheherazade of *One Thousand and One Nights* fame, which, of course, is more than coincidence. Grossman has said that after Uri's death, he returned to writing *To the End of the Land* as "a way of fighting against the gravity of grief . . . a way of choosing life." This is essentially what Scheherazade does in *One Thousand and One Nights*. King Shahryar, embittered by his queen's betrayal, has her executed. Believing now that all women are deceitful, he marries a virgin every night, only to kill her at dawn before she has a chance to betray him. Scheherazade, his latest bride, enthralls him night after night with tantalizing stories that arouse his curiosity and empathy. Eventually she not only heals the king but also saves her own life. For her, as for Ora, stories are a means of survival, an affirmation of life.

To the End of the Land, like Scheherazade's story, is made up of numerous tales told in order to survive, and perchance to change the deadly grip of an external force. One could almost divide the novel into tales that Ora tells Avram during their long walk across Galilee: Ofer's Tale, Adam's Tale, The Tale of the Well, The Tale of the Bed, Ilan's Tale. And, as in *Nights*, here is a frame story, one that begins with the meeting and flourishing of a deep love and unique bond among three teenagers, Avram, Ora, and Ilan.

DEAR BABA, I HAVE NEWS for you, and, these days, very little news is good news. We are plagued by a coronavirus that originated in Wuhan, China, and has now become a global pandemic. In January 2020 the first cases were reported, and, since then, this deadly virus has spread around the world. At first, this seemed like just another faraway news story—terrible but not yet felt; somewhere in the back of my mind, but not yet actual. I first felt its presence in a concrete manner following a trip I took in February to Kuwait and Bahrain to give a speech. As I prepared to board my flight back to the States in the Bahrain airport, I noticed a number of people wearing medical masks, an ominous sign that something was not quite right. Two weeks after my return, in early March, the first cases of the virus were detected in DC.

We now have a new vocabulary to describe our new reality: *lockdown* means staying at home unless we need to go out for essentials such as groceries. *Social distancing* means keeping six feet apart from others, because the virus attacks mainly through inhalation. This also means that we cannot see our children or friends except through virtual reality. Now, three weeks after the lockdown, I still cannot fathom what all this means for us, for the country, and for the world.

BABA JAN, I SO RELATE to Ora and her desperate attempt to keep Ofer alive. Moments of extreme violence demand moments of extreme compassion. Ora uses love, stories, and magical thinking to ward off harm and danger. Sometimes a book, like *To the End of the Land*, gets under my skin and won't leave me. Even when I was not actually reading the book, I kept it with me. I carried it from my bedroom to my living room, placing it on the side table next to me while watching television. I carried it to doctor appointments, in the Metro, to coffee shops. Just having it in my backpack gave me a sense of security, protection. Reading it, I was transported to anxiety-filled moments in the Islamic Republic of Iran when I'd carried around other books like talismans: Heinrich Böll's *The Clown*, Emily Brontë's *Wuthering Heights*, Gabriel García Márquez's *One Hundred Years of Solitude*, Marcel Proust's *In Search of the Lost Time*.

ANYONE WHO KNOWS ABOUT GROSSMAN is aware that he has publicly called for an end to the Israeli government's occupation of Palestinian territories. What is miraculous, however, is that although these sentiments are reflected in his novel, they do not form the foundation of the novel. They are woven into the story's fabric in a way that simultaneously speaks to and transcends politics. There is an anguished and precarious beauty in *To the End of the Land*; against the callousness and violence of political and social realities, this beauty becomes an act of rebellion. Negating the ideological jargon of politicians and defying the deep political, social, and cultural divide that has been imposed on the people of this land, Grossman creates a universal space and a set of common values through which both the Israeli and Palestinian peoples can experience their shared humanity and their desire for a decent, dignified life. As Robert Alter, an American literary critic, says in his beautiful review of *To the End of the Land*, Ora does not perceive the world as a Zionist or anti-Zionist; instead, she sees it as a mother. And as a mother, when her first son, Adam, returns from the war, she knows instinctively that those who go to war never come back the same—that their former selves are lost forever.

War and conflict take their toll on everyone. Baba jan, have you thought of how you would deal with a child who has just discovered the meaning of the word *enemy*? What does it do to the psyche of a six-year-old to be confronted with the notion that there are people who are perfect strangers to him and yet want to destroy him? At one point in the novel, Ora thinks back to when Ofer, at age six, asked her one day in a state of panic, "Mommy, who's against us?" He continues, "Who hates us in the world?" Ofer is consumed with fear at the thought of Israel's many foreign enemies. To calm the boy, Ora bundles him up and takes him to the site of Israel's Armored Corps to show him its tanks, assuring her son that there are many more where these came from. Ironic, of course, because Ora is against the war.

Dear Baba, you would think the answer to Ofer's question is easy: Arabs, especially Palestinians, are the enemy. They are the ones Israelis go to war with, they are the ones who

plant bombs in Israeli buses, restaurants, and public spaces.
But things are more complicated, because when we leave the
generalized and formulaic language of politicians and their
wars, we discover that there are so many different kinds
of people categorized under that one word, *enemy*. I know
exactly what Grossman means when he says, "In a disaster
zone, of course, or in a prolonged war, the tendency of the
hawkish sides is to minimize and deny the human aspect
of the enemy, to flatten it into a stereotype or a collection
of prejudices." Baba jan, I now live in a democratic society,
and I know that even in a democracy that is not at war with
a foreign power, that does not live in occupied territories, a
tyrannical mindset can invent enemies and "flatten" people
"into a stereotype or a collection of prejudices."

In *To the End of the Land*, Avram's Egyptian torturers beat
and torture him, withholding food and water, pulling out his
fingernails and toenails, and, as Grossman describes, they hang
him "by his hands from the ceiling and whipped the soles of
his feet with rubber clubs, and hooked electrical wires to his
testicles, and nipples and tongue, and raped him." The torture
is horrendous, and yet through most of it, Avram manages
to hold on to hope in the form of a small act of kindness by a
warden, a bird chirping, and, above all, a piece of writing he
has been working on. But eventually his spirit is broken, as we
witness Avram's truly terrifying experience of being buried
alive while an Egyptian officer takes photos. As Grossman
observes: "Avram no longer wanted to live in a world where
such a thing was possible, where a person stood photographing
someone being buried alive, and Avram let go of his life and
died." He is finally released and returns home, but he is so

shell shocked by the experience that he does not even feel any anger toward his torturers. He does not physically die, but he gives up on his love for living, and, with that, he also gives up his writing. Baba, I cannot get the passage describing Avram's burial out of my head. Time and again I read it, wondering about the reality Grossman had experienced in order to produce those lines.

I think it takes a great deal of generosity and understanding, as well as insight, to acknowledge that despite such savagery, the Egyptian people as a whole cannot be equated with these torturers, much in the same way that Iran cannot be equated with the crimes committed by the Islamic regime, and America cannot be equated with the My Lai massacre in Vietnam or the torture at Abu Ghraib. Each is responsible for the atrocities but is not equated with them. Once we recognize this, we have a different view of our enemy. At one point during the war, Ilan recalls an Egyptian pilot whose plane was on fire parachuting to the ground. The Egyptian soldiers all rushed toward him, embraced him, and appeared to shield him from attack from the Israeli stronghold. He tells Ora he had "never felt how much they were real, living people, flesh and blood and soul, as sharply as he felt now, watching them hug their pilot friend."

I remember you once telling me that one of the most difficult challenges in your life had been to understand your enemies, to humanize them. It was easier, more straightforward to turn them into demons with no ambiguities attached. Didn't you once say that you often wondered if your archenemy the prime minister loved his two daughters the way you loved Mohammad and me?

That love, you said, might have been what you and he
had in common. When Grossman humanizes his enemy,
he creates some of the most touching scenes in the novel.
During the war, Avram tells Ora he loved listening to the
enemy officers and admits he was more interested in gossip,
intrigues, and jabs among them than military secrets—in
other words, you might say, he was most interested in the
feelings and emotions that were common to all of us. Once,
he eavesdropped on two radio operators from the Second
Army and realized that they were in love and "were sending
each other innuendos over the official network." He adds,
"That's the kind of thing I was looking for." "The human
voice?" Ora suggests. To me, Baba jan, these human moments
seem so ordinary—mundane, almost—and yet have such a
miraculous effect, especially in times of extreme trauma,
when we need to be reminded of our humanity.

I was telling my friend Shirin the other day how this virus
and lockdown have made me even more aware of the fact that
in order to remain human, we need the human connection. I
told her how, during the eight-year Iran-Iraq War, I felt close
to and empathetic toward the Iraqi people. I was sure that
their feelings about the war were akin to ours: an atrocity
created by two tyrannical leaders. I had the same feeling
toward the Iraqi nation during America's disastrous 2003 war
against Iraq.

Dear Baba, I believe that if for nothing else, you would
have loved *To the End of the Land* for its memorable
characters. One such character is an Arab Israeli named
Sami, who owns a cab company and has been driving Ora's
family around for years. Ora and Sami are on friendly, even

intimate, terms. Ora loves talking to Sami about his family and clan, the intrigues at the town council—even about the woman he had loved at fifteen and had continued loving after his marriage. It broke my heart to see how it takes only one incident, one act of carelessness, to almost destroy all they had shared together.

At the very beginning of the novel, Ora calls Sami to drive her and Ofer to the war zone, forgetting carelessly that he is an Arab and will be driving Ofer to the zone so that he can fight and perhaps kill Arabs. That same day, she again calls on Sami, this time to drive her to pick up Avram, and she helps Sami take a very sick Palestinian boy to a secret makeshift hospital for illegal Arabs in Israel. Later, thinking about the makeshift refugee hospital while walking with Avram, she realizes "what Sami was going through when he saw those injured, beaten people." Ora vows to apologize to her Arab friend upon her return, "because," Grossman writes, "if he and she cannot make up after one bad day, then maybe there really is no chance that the greater conflict will be resolved." Baba jan, I wonder if the author is saying here that the damage to their relationship was done long before Sami and Ora even met, by a force over which they had no control?

DEAR BABA, I WAS TALKING to Shirin about what Trump shares with the leaders of the Islamic Republic: cruelty, incompetence, and a reckless disregard for the lives of the citizens of his country. In Iran, when air raid sirens warned us of an imminent attack, it was a signal that we should retreat to

bomb shelters. But as you know, we had nowhere to go. The
government never *built* any shelters, and the sirens became
a mockery of the Iranian people. We'd been left on our own
without any protection.

Of course, the same thing is happening now across the
globe during the coronavirus pandemic. I never imagined that
I would experience this same feeling of fear and helplessness
living in the United States as I did in Iran under the Islamic
Republic. But frighteningly, it is similar. For as far as the
federal government is concerned, nothing terrible is happening
in this country. Trump keeps telling us that the virus is not
that bad, that it will magically go away, that we will get back
to normal, and that we need not worry. How can he be so
careless with the lives of more than three hundred million
Americans? That, of course, is a rhetorical question. I already
know the answer.

DOESN'T IT AMAZE YOU HOW intimate we become with our
enemies, how much they reveal about us, how complicit we
become in one another's wars? Baba jan, are you familiar with
the British poet Wilfred Owen, a veteran of World War I? I
read him in college, and he has stayed with me not so much
because of the beauty of his verse but because of the startling
truths he reveals about war. He has said, "All a poet can do
today is warn," adding, "That is why the true poets must be
truthful." Owen's "Dulce et Decorum Est" directly refutes
what he calls "the old lie"—a sort of modern echo of Plato's
noble lie that "it is sweet and fitting to die for one's country."
In the poem, the narrator is addressed by the man he has

killed in battle. Owen brings out the terrible intimacy that forms between mortal enemies, and, in doing so, he rescues the humanity of both parties:

> I am the enemy you killed, my friend.
> I knew you in this dark: for so you frowned
> Yesterday through me as you jabbed and killed.

Dear Baba, reading Grossman, I am reminded of Owen, whose poem evokes a paradox that Grossman similarly seems to be facing: it is possible to love one's country and to risk one's life by going to war for that country, while at the same time hating the war and blaming one's country for it. Often, the most astute critics are those who were prepared to sacrifice their lives for their homeland. War involves courage and sacrifice, but it also forces us to see ourselves, our enemies, and humanity differently. Winning or losing is only one aspect of war. You may feel hate for your enemy and hold a gun to his head while he simultaneously holds a gun to yours. But you may also come to the realization in this moment that you have both been diminished and dehumanized.

It is as Grossman says in his essay "Writing in the Dark": "I try not to shield myself from the legitimacy and the suffering of my enemy, or from the tragedy and complexity of his life, or from his mistakes and crimes or from knowing what I myself am doing to him. Nor do I shelter myself from the surprising similarities I discover between him and me." He goes on to say, "I write. And all at once, I am no longer doomed to face this absolute, false, suffocating dichotomy—this inhuman choice between 'victim' and 'aggressor,' without any third, more human option." Dear Baba, that "third, more human option" doesn't always work, for sometimes the suffering caused by our enemies is overwhelming. But then, that option seems to be our best option.

TALKING OF CHOOSING THE "THIRD OPTION," I am reminded of the joint project of the late Palestinian American scholar Edward Said and the Argentina-born Israeli conductor Daniel Barenboim. In 1999 they created an orchestra named after Johann Wolfgang Goethe's collection of poems (inspired by the Persian classical poet Hāfez) called *West-Eastern Divan.* The unique characteristic of this orchestra was that its members came from diverse backgrounds; mainly from countries that considered themselves political adversaries or even enemies. They came from Palestine and Israel, other Arab countries, and Iran. As Said explained: "Humanism is the only—I would go so far as saying the final—resistance we have against the inhuman practices and injustices that disfigure human history. Separation between peoples is not a solution for any of the problems that divide peoples. And certainly ignorance of the other provides no help whatsoever. Cooperation and coexistence of the kind that music lived as we have lived, performed, shared, and loved it together might be."

Barenboim, who apart from Israeli has other nationalities, explained to the *Los Angeles Times* the nonmusical idea behind the orchestra: "The Divan was conceived as a project against ignorance. . . . It is absolutely essential for people to get to know the other, to understand what the other thinks and feels, without necessarily agreeing with it."

OTHER POETS AND WRITERS WHO, like Grossman, have gone to war have expressed this sentiment: the dissonance between serving their country while opposing war itself. World War I brought this discrepancy to the fore. The British poet Siegfried Sassoon, who also fought in that war, had blistering criticism for those who celebrated it. In his poem "Suicide in the Trenches," he says:

> *You smug-faced crowds with kindling eye*
> *Who cheer when soldier lads march by*
> *Sneak home and pray you never know*
> *The hell where youth and laughter go.*

For Grossman, as for Owen and Sassoon, the homeland is a place of war, and ordinary citizens experience war's presence in their daily lives. This is not the case in modern America, where wars have been fought on foreign soil. For American soldiers today, the disconnect between their experiences of war and those of the country they return to must feel insurmountable. The feelings of isolation and alienation they contend with must be immense.

DEAR BABA, I THINK YOU would enjoy reading the young American novelist and writer Elliot Ackerman. He is a former marine who served five tours of duty in Iraq and Afghanistan and received the Silver Star, the Bronze Star for Valor, and the Purple Heart. Most of his writing is about war—not just warfare itself but also the people he encountered in lands where he fought. Like Grossman, Ackerman is curious about his enemies, getting to know them through writing about them. His first novel, *Green on Blue*, published in 2015, focuses on the tender relationship between a young Afghani boy named Aziz and his older brother, Ali. The siblings lose their stable family life when their parents are killed and, throughout the book, they struggle to survive the brutalities and violence of a war imposed upon them. Ackerman's 2019 book, *Places and Names: On War, Revolution and Returning*, is a memoir of conflicts he has fought in and their aftermath. In its pages, Ackerman writes about an encounter with a Syrian man named Abu Hassar, who fought with al-Qaeda in Mesopotamia and is now living in a refugee camp in Turkey. The meeting between these two men—an American marine and a former terrorist—is like something straight out of one of Grossman's novels. When they are introduced, Abu Hassar takes a vial of perfume from the pocket of his Adidas sweatshirt, dabs some of it on his own hand, and then takes Ackerman by the wrist and rubs the perfume from his palm onto Ackerman's. He follows this act by explaining, "The Prophet says there are three things one must never refuse: a good pillow, good yogurt, and good perfume." Sometimes the cliché "life is full of surprises" is a good thing: this is not the sort of behavior that we would typically expect from a former al-Qaeda recruit.

Dear Baba, you once said to me we might survive the Iran-Iraq War physically, but how we would survive it psychologically was another matter. War amplifies our extremes, leaving little room for the complexities and contradictions that make us human. In his memoirs, Ackerman confronts these contradictions and tries to make sense of them, much as Grossman tries to do in his own work. We would consider Abu Hassar to be a terrorist, and during America's war in Iraq, he was Ackerman's mortal enemy, yet here they are, sitting at a table and talking about their families and war experiences over lunch, tea, and baklava, with the help of Ackerman's translator, a former Syrian democracy activist named Abed.

They try to understand each other rather than to judge and condemn. They talk about their children (Ackerman has two; Abu Hassar, three), their countries (both failed in their wars), their biggest fears during the war (Ackerman's was getting lost; Abu Hassar's was *not* getting killed but getting arrested), and why they each went off to fight in a war that he fundamentally disagreed with. Ackerman explains his decision to enlist and fight this way: when your country goes to war, you have a choice to join or not. "And you'll always remember what you chose," he says, adding, "I don't regret my choice, but maybe I regret being asked to choose." I wonder if David Grossman, too, regrets being asked to choose.

Baba, I must tell you that I relate to this dilemma. As an Iranian citizen, when I lived in Iran I felt torn between wanting to support and defend my country, while at the same time knowing that I was against the war between Iraq and the Islamic regime. I felt that it was the Iranian regime's war, not mine, not the Iranian people's. Abu Hassar describes a similar feeling in his conversation with Ackerman. After America's invasion of Iraq in 2003, as an Arab and a Muslim, he considered it his duty to fight. This seems to have been the same reason that Ofer went to war in *To the End of the Land*.

Not because he believed in the war or liked the idea of war, but because of loyalty. Because his country called for it. Dear Baba, it seems that no matter what you do, whether you go to war or refuse to do so, the contradiction and the dilemma remain.

There is a scene in Ackerman's memoirs, at the heart of this encounter, that I like very much: Abed the translator goes to the restroom, and the two men who do not speak each other's language sit silently. Then Ackerman opens his notebook and draws the Euphrates River. Abu Hassar takes the pencil from him and draws the straight borderline between Iraq and Syria. Next, Ackerman takes back the pencil and writes, "al-Qaim"—the name of an Iraqi town along the border that his former foe has drawn. Abu Hassar then writes a date, and Ackerman adds his own date. They continue adding to the map the places where they had been fighting.

"Our hands now chase each other's around the map, mimicking the way we'd once chased each other around this country," Ackerman writes. To his relief, one thing they discover is that "we have many places that overlap, nearly all of them, but we don't have a single date that does." Perhaps he felt relief that they did not have to confront each other in any of these locations.

At one point, Ackerman feels that "Abu Hassar has hit on a unifying thread between us: friendships born out of conflict, the strongest we've ever known." He adds, "I think that's why I sought out Abu Hassar: to see if that thread binds two people who've fought against each other." Ackerman wonders why Abu Hassar has agreed to meet him and decides, "Maybe he, like me, has become tired of learning the ways we are different. Maybe he wishes to learn some of the ways we are the same." Before they met Abu Hassar, Ackerman and Abed had agreed not to tell him that Ackerman had been a marine. Instead, Ackerman would introduce himself as a journalist. But now they decide to tell him the truth. Upon hearing this, Abu Hassar pours a glass of water and hands it to Ackerman.

In many ways, Baba jan, wouldn't things have been easier if these two men had discovered that they could not communicate? That they could not relate as human beings, with families, feelings, and senses of humor? Had this been the case, we would all have been saved from many questions, complications, and contradictions. Ackerman went to war and served his country faithfully—in fact, heroically—but along with the medals and memories, he brought back the realization that "those" people were people after all. He came back with a burning curiosity to know the enemy, to experience them as individuals, as human beings—which, I believe, is the main reason he wrote *Places and Names*. It is to avoid such complications that we polarize and dehumanize those whom we consider "other." Sometimes we have no choice but to go to war; to kill the enemy or be killed. But our broader understanding of the world need not be so black and white, which is why we need narrative and the understanding that stories bring us. As I read and reread the scene between Ackerman and Abu Hassar, I was reminded of a quote from David Grossman: "To write about the enemy means, primarily, to think about the enemy, and this is a requirement for anyone who has an enemy, even if he is absolutely convinced of his own justness and the enemy's malice and cruelty. To think (or to write) about the enemy does not necessarily mean to justify him."

This, dear Baba, is important: understanding does *not* mean justifying, does *not* even mean forgiving. Even if your sole aim

is to defeat the enemy, you must know him in order to defeat
him. I am interested to know: How would you have felt had
you not been given a trial, had you not been exonerated?

At one point, Ackerman tells Abu Hassar a story: During
World War I, in 1914, it snowed on Christmas Day, and in
the cold the British and German soldiers climbed out of their
trenches at the small Belgium town of Mons. They spent that
whole day exchanging small gifts and playing soccer. When
Abu Hassar asks what they did the next day, Ackerman
replies, "Went back to their trenches and killed each other for
another four years."

For me, Ackerman's writing, like Grossman's, offers a ritual
cleansing of the soul. War, by nature, dehumanizes the enemy.
Story gives the enemy a voice, forcing us to confront him
as a human being, to look him in the eye. And through this
process, we restore our own humanity.

DEAR BABA, I KEEP HAVING flashbacks to wartime in Iran. That
same eerie feeling akin to dread that I had then, I have now.
One thing that the rockets and this deadly virus have in
common is that their fallout is both expected and unexpected.
In the back of our minds, we know they might strike at any
moment, like death, which we know will arrive sooner or later.

One thing I must tell you, a piece of good news—in fact,
the best possible kind of news—and yet now it is tinged with
anxiety and dread: Negar and Kelli, Dara's wife, are both
pregnant! Yes, congratulations! You are going to be a great-
grandfather! I remember my own two pregnancies and the
secret bond I felt with this as yet not wholly formed being
inside me. I felt excitement, tenderness, and the overwhelming

desire to protect this being at all costs. I also felt anxious about how Negar and Kelli would fare during the pandemic.

I flash back to the day I gave birth to Negar. After they had brought me from surgery to my room, I opened my eyes and saw you standing close to the end of my bed, your gaze fixed on me. You were smiling. Now, despite my anxieties, I too am smiling.

AS I SEE IT, *To the End of the Land* is in part about what Grossman calls living in "the disaster zone," constantly on guard, "clenched both physically and emotionally." You and I, having lived in the Islamic Republic, know what it means to live in a disaster zone. Grossman, in an essay, clarifies that he is not talking "politics" but wants to show the internal changes and process those living in the disaster zone go through. He also wants to show the role of literature and writing "in a climate as lethal as the one we live in."

Living in a disaster zone, as Ora and her family do, focuses our whole attention and diverts us from the everyday joys and pains of living. I keep thinking of another piece Grossman wrote called "The Desire to be Gisella," which appears in his book *Writing in the Dark*. In it, he explains why every day during the first two years of the second intifada (September 2000–February 2005) he went to his office to work on a story he was writing about a man and a woman who spend a whole night in a car on "an intense and turbulent journey." Baba jan, I think he must be talking about his novella "Frenzy." When asked why he ignored the political situation and the intifada in his story, Grossman tells us that his characters turn their backs on the political situation because "they instinctively feel that this 'situation' may cause them to miss out on the most important things in their lives." He goes on to say, "They feel that because of the 'situation' and its terrors, they barely have the time or energy left over to inquire into the greater questions of human existence, and their own private little existence, which happens to have been tossed into the disaster zone of the Middle East."

I have the same feeling about Negar's and Kelli's pregnancies: I want to enjoy the moment, one of anticipation and joy, yet both the political atmosphere and the pandemic interfere and replace joy with a sense of gloom, a grayness. To focus on the simple everyday events of life becomes an existential way of resisting the disaster zone. Grossman writes, "I have deliberately assumed the calm and sober language of the witness, not the lamenting tones of the victim or the irate voice of someone who seeks revenge." Baba jan, I believe this is why we need what Nabokov calls the third eye of imagination, in order to see the world both as it is and to transcend the everyday in order to understand it.

Dear Baba, my memories of the eight-year-long war between the Islamic Republic of Iran and Iraq are saturated with fear, with the anticipation of disaster. Even during the hours when there were no bombs falling, in the back of my mind, I was always waiting for them to drop, hearing their heavy *thump* and experiencing a fear that shaped even my smallest acts: taking the ice cream out of the freezer, combing Negar's hair, lying in bed reading while the dust mites floated through the air. In my mind, no moment was free of bombs and missiles. Living in a totalitarian society is similar to living in a disaster zone. Individuals experience a different kind of fear: the constant anxiety that the way you look, the way you act, the way you think or feel is illegal and punishable. At any moment, you could be reprimanded, arrested, or jailed simply because of who you are. Do you remember those panicked phone calls that we would make to each other every time a bomb dropped in Tehran, to make sure that the other person had been spared? And then, of course, came the guilt of knowing that someone else's loved one had been sacrificed.

BABA JAN, YESTERDAY I WAS talking on the phone with Shirin in Iran, and she asked me, "Are you enjoying your moment?" When I asked her what she meant, she explained that I have always made dire predictions about political and cultural conditions, and now all of my predictions had come true—not just in Iran, but also where I currently live, America. "You guys in America," she said, "have been going from bad to worse, and now you are moving from worse to worst!" "So," she added sardonically, "enjoy your moment while you can!" I told her I had a funny feeling that this moment both in the US and Iran was going to stretch into years, so I would have ample time to enjoy myself.

Although she said this in jest, I wish I could enjoy something, anything, about "my moment." But I am going from bad to worse myself, on my way to the worst. I have become so intolerant of Trump and his enablers. Everything for me somehow leads to Trump. When friends ask how I am doing, I usually respond, "How are any of us doing under present conditions?" I find any excuse I can to rage against the current administration. It is not just about Trump but also about the fact that he brings out the worst and the most extreme in both his supporters and in some among the opposition. He certainly brings out the worst in me.

I try to imagine what life would be like if Trump gets reelected in 2020. It reminds me of times back in Iran when I would get so fed up that I'd try to wish the regime away. I'm not sure why I thought this was a good use of my time, and I am amazed at my own level of intolerance. Here I am, preaching on the importance of understanding one's enemy, and yet I cannot even bring myself listen to Trump for two minutes. This is the problem: you can become so engrossed with your "enemy" that you lose all objectivity and become paralyzed, unable to think or understand beyond hate. The enemy controls your actions, which are mostly reactions. This is how your enemy gets under your skin, becoming so intimate, lurking in the deepest recesses of your mind. I recognize now the heroism of writers such as Grossman, Ackerman, Owen, and Sassoon, who refuse to give in to their rage and hatred and instead try to channel it toward understanding, no matter how bitter the results might be. Hatred and rage without direction dehumanize not just the enemy but oneself. It eats away at you and brings about a kind of blindness.

Baba jan, I have to tell you this: in one of these moments of rage, I remembered a brilliant book I had read a while before. It is a poetic and heartbreaking novel, *Gate of the Sun*, by celebrated Lebanese writer Elias Khoury, who was awarded the Palestine Prize. Like *To the End of the Land*, *Gate of the Sun* is about life in a "disaster zone" and ways of dealing with the enemy, only it does so from the Palestinian perspective. I would have loved to teach the two books together.

It is the inner poetry of *Gate of the Sun* that makes it so heartbreakingly beautiful. At one point, the narrator, a certain Dr. Khalil Ayyoub, living in a Palestinian refugee camp at Shatila in 1995, on the outskirts of Beirut, describes poetry as "words we use to heal our shame, our sorrow, our longing. It's a cover. The poet wraps us up in words so our souls don't fall to pieces. Poetry is against death—it's both sickness and cure, the bare soul and its clothes. I'm cold now, so I take refuge in poetry, hiding my head in it and asking it to cover me." Don't you feel as if you could have said these words or had this feeling?

Baba, you must prepare yourself for being a bit disturbed and uncomfortable when reading Elias Khoury, who draws you in and holds you but offers little comfort. Beauty and tenderness, yes, but not comfort—if you are looking for that, you have chosen the wrong writer. As I read *Gate of the Sun*, the novel seemed to unfold in parallel with the current political situation; I felt like I was walking a tightrope high above the ground, struggling to keep my balance and not fall.

Like Grossman's Ora, who uses stories to prevent her son Ofer from getting killed in war, Khalil is telling stories to his mentor, Yunes al-Asadi, an elderly Palestinian fighter and hero who is in a coma. He hopes to keep his patient alive by telling him tales from Palestine since the 1948 Arab-Israeli War. The stories cover the lives and deaths of Palestinians, dislocated, constantly on the move, constantly on the brink of death. In short sketches, Khalil individualizes every character by telling and expanding on a crucial moment in that character's life. Sometimes he tells the same story from different points of view. "I'm scared of history that has only one version," he explains. "History has dozens of versions, and for it to ossify into one only leads to death." It is not only Yunes that Khalil tries to save from death through his stories but also those Palestinians who appear in his yarns, followed by violence and desperation.

At one point in the book, Khalil says, "Words are wounds." And Khoury himself has said that the Arabic linguistic origins of *word* is "wound." Khoury sees writing as an act in which you write with your wounds in order to heal your wounds. You can imagine how it feels to read a book that uses words as wounds; you can't help but feel both lacerated and cleansed.

BABA JAN, SINCE WE CAN do little more than leave the house for groceries in the pandemic, yesterday we had a "meeting" with the kids via Zoom. I keep forgetting how much you don't know about the world we live in now. You have never heard of Zoom, for instance, which defines itself as "a remote conferencing service that allows colleagues to hold virtual meetings with one another from anywhere with an internet connection." Video meetings through the computer. Those science-fiction films and books you and I used to see and read have come true! Many people are excited that, during these times when we cannot meet face-to-face, we can at least use technology to connect, and, of course, they are right. We even had a baby shower for both Negar and Kelli on Zoom. But these Zoom meetings with the kids later made me depressed. It made the distance and the impossibility of meeting in real life more palpable. Their presence on virtual reality intensifies their absence in real life. I feel nostalgic for them even as I watch them on my computer screen. I am missing out on so much, including Negar's pregnancy.

This is one difference between the war experience and

the experience of life in the pandemic. During the war, we became physically close not just with family and friends, but also with strangers whom we might have otherwise ignored had things been normal. Now it's quite the opposite: we have to treat loved ones and acquaintances as if they pose a threat—the threat of infection—and we must try to keep a physical distance. It is strange to pass people in the street now and to know that we must avoid them—that even a brief conversation could be dangerous.

You remember, Baba jan, the movie nights we had back during the war, when sometimes as many as twenty or so people would gather in someone's home to watch the forbidden videos of either classic films or the latest movies. Usually people stayed the night because of the blackouts. I remember one such occasion at our place—I think it was directors John Ford and Howard Hawks night—when almost every room in our apartment was filled with people who stayed the night. Early the next morning, I was in the kitchen with some friends, drinking coffee and eating toast with cream and honey, when we heard the heavy *thump*, and the windows started rattling. There was a moment of utter silence, and then people started queuing for the phone, to make sure their loved ones were okay. At these times, I always instinctively ran toward our children's rooms, as if my presence would create an impenetrable barrier that no rocket or bomb could destroy.

BABA, THINKING OF OUR TIME in the Islamic Republic, I realize that one result of trauma, of living in a disaster zone, is that victim and oppressor are joined at the hip. As a victim, you allow yourself to be defined by your oppressor, accepting

your perpetual state of victimhood. How does one avoid
being defined as a victim under those circumstances? Both
Grossman and Khoury come up with a surprising answer:
know thy enemy! Acknowledge your enemy.

Baba jan, I don't think that such an answer is a surprise to
you, as you certainly knew and acknowledged your enemy
while spending time in jail. Yes, of course, know thy enemy,
for knowledge is power. But imagine when you are enmeshed
in war, or when, as in today's America, you work yourself up
into a warlike state where the political lines are drawn, and
there is no doubt as to who the good and the bad guys are.
Under such circumstances, knowing your enemy, which means
understanding him, accepting him as another human being,
becomes an explosive concept.

Grossman writes, "I try not to shield myself from the
legitimacy and the suffering of my enemy, or from the tragedy
and complexity of his life, or from his mistakes and crimes, or
from knowing what I myself am doing to him. Nor do I shelter
myself from the surprising similarities between him and me."
It is these "surprising similarities" that Khalil is interested in.
He claims he has discovered the "secret of war." He believes
this secret is the mirror: your enemy is your mirror! "I know
no one will agree with me," he says, "and they'll say I talk like
this because I'm afraid, but it's not true. If you're afraid, you
don't say your enemy is your mirror, you run away from him."
To some, this might sound like an outlandish claim, but when
you're so polarized that there is no room for contact, for any
form of discourse, you can easily become the other side of the
coin to your enemy. You might disagree on issues but adopt
the same attitude, act in the same manner. That is the state of
mind Wilfred Owen addresses in his poem "Dulce et Decorum

Est." "I want to say," says Khalil, "that the real war begins when your enemy becomes your mirror so that you kill him in order to kill yourself."

For Dr. Ayyoub, "Massacres are not supposed to happen, and if they happen, they must be condemned and their perpetrators arrested and taken to court." Notice, Baba jan, he does not say *we* should take revenge on the perpetrators, or that some people can commit massacres but others cannot. Massacres are evil no matter who commits them. He documents meticulously the suffering inflicted upon the Palestinians by the Israelis but uses the same logic when he speaks of the killing of Israeli athletes at the Munich Olympics in 1972, telling Yunes: "I know what you think of that kind of operation, and I know you were one of the few who dared take a stand against the hijacking of airplanes, the operations abroad, and the killing of civilians."

Obviously, we cannot condemn the actions of our oppressors and then go ahead and repeat them ourselves. We must be different and act differently—that I learned from you. Khalil reminds himself and Yunes of the tragedy of Damour, a Christian city just south of Beirut that was attacked in 1976 by Saika, a pro-Syrian Palestinian militia that killed about four hundred civilians. Later, it was decided to house the refugees from Tal al-Za'atar camp, themselves victims of the siege by extremist Christian groups, in Damour, now that it had been cleansed of its Christian inhabitants. Khalil says, "I thought that's what the Jews did to us, and we're going to do the same to the people of Damour? It's not possible; it's a crime." It is incidents like this that lead Khalil tell his mentor, "Truly, Yunes my son, the only thing people fear is themselves. You told me the only thing you were afraid of when you crossed the border was your own shadow, which would stretch out on the ground and follow you."

You see, Baba jan, I feel this is so very important because such a worldview rescues us from our self-righteousness, and what I see today in both countries I have called home is a heavy dose of self-righteousness without much humility or doubt.

"Everything foolish we do, we blame on the Jews," Khalil complains. To be a victim is to abdicate responsibility, to in effect give up most of all on yourself. "All war stories have evaporated; all that's left are the massacres. Are we imitating our enemies, or are they imitating their executioners?" It is when you cast off the mantle of victimhood that you become a menace, a danger to your oppressor. It is intriguing that in order to cease being a victim, you must accept responsibility for who you are and who you might become—thus, ironically, acknowledging your enemy and the fact that you might be like him rescues you from victimhood. It is a transfer of power, when you realize the enemy is not the all-powerful, omniscient presence controlling everything we do. We have a choice; therefore we are free. We can choose to become like the enemy—or not.

FOR KHOURY, IT IS PARTICULARLY painful that those who are now Palestinians' enemies were once victims of the most horrendous crimes of the twentieth century. He empathizes with those victims and their fate. With amazing generosity of spirit, the author reminds us of their enemy's own tragedy. In a much-quoted passage, Khalil tells his comatose mentor, "You and I and every human being on the face of the planet should have known and not stood by in silence, should have prevented that beast from destroying its victims in that barbarian, unprecedented manner. Not because the victims were Jews but because their death meant the death of humanity within us." For him, what we do on an individual level can have universal resonance. He asks Yunes, "In the faces of those people being driven to slaughter, didn't you see something resembling your own?"

Dear Baba, as you can see, Khoury is set on complicating matters: victims can become perpetrators, which is why it is important that they know they can change roles with their enemy, and perpetrators could have been victims themselves at one time. In an interview with the Israeli daily *Yediot Aharonot*, he said, "When I was working on this book, I discovered that the 'other' is the mirror of the I. And given that I am writing about a half century of Palestinian experience, it is impossible to read this experience otherwise than in the mirror of the Israeli 'other.' Therefore, when I was writing this novel, I put a lot of effort into trying to take apart not only the Palestinian stereotype but also the Israeli stereotype as it appears in Arab literature and especially in the Palestinian literature of Ghassan Kanafani [1936–1972, writer and one of the leaders of the Popular Front for the Liberation of Palestine who was assassinated by the Israeli secret police, Mossad], for example, or even of Emile Habibi [1922–1996, a Palestinian Israeli writer and member of the Knesset]. The Israeli is not only the policeman or the occupier, he is the 'other,' who also has a human experience, and we need to read this experience. Our reading of their experience is a mirror to our reading of the Palestinian experience." In the book,

Khalil says, "Them and us. As you see, they've become like us, and we've become like them. We no longer possess any other memory."

Having been a victim does not justify making victims of others. Nahila, Yunes's wife, tells her military interrogator: "You were tormented, but your torment doesn't give you the right to torment us." It is as simple as that.

DEAR BABA, IT IS BEAUTIFUL the way that Grossman, in *To the End of the Land*, turns a political question into an existential one: in order to live decently in indecent times, can we afford to treat others, even our enemies, indecently? His answer— no—is at the core of Grossman's worldview and serves as the basis for *To the End of the Land*. It turns out that living a decent life is the most challenging task of all.

Returning to the world of facts for a moment, the imperative of behaving decently toward our enemy has led to positive, if obviously imperfect, results throughout history, such as the Geneva Conventions, the League of Nations, the United Nations, the Universal Declaration of Human Rights, the International Criminal Court, and Mandela's Truth and Reconciliation. In each of these cases, against the backdrop of war and violence, the attempt was made to treat everyone, including enemies from both sides, fairly and justly. Baba, do you see a contradiction here? What I mean is, war is based on the fact that there is no fair or just way of encountering the enemy, while, at the same time, it is demanded that we be fair and just. Despite the contradiction, the demand is to safeguard our essential human sense of dignity and decency, even against an enemy that has no such sense, for it seems that to lose one's dignity and decency is tantamount to losing one's life.

This attitude is implied in most of Grossman's work. He claims, "Behind the armor of fear, indifference, hatred, and the constriction of the soul; behind everything that languishes within each one of us as these difficult years go by; behind all the fortified wall—there is a *human being*." In order to see this human being behind the armor, we must create a domain that is separate; an alternate, fictional reality. We need to communicate in a different language, one devoid of generalizations, categorizations, and what he calls "nationalization." Thinking of *To the End of the Land*, I think in metaphors. And I understand how he uses the magic of language, of narrative, as a kind of protection and a protest. This writing is an act of defiance against the absolute silences of death, against the generalizations that always mimic death by erasing the details, the individual, and the particular. One way of resisting war and death is remembering life, in all its trivialities. And being tender. This is the first thing that war and oppression take away from you: tenderness.

IN *TO THE END OF THE LAND*, Ora asks these questions of herself, her family, Avram, and, finally, of the book's readers: What about simple human decency? Is life worth living if we are forced to abandon that? We faced these same questions in life under the Islamic Republic, and my heart goes out to Ora. We encounter so many wars in this one book, and so many enemies, but perhaps the most significant of them is Ora's war against complacency and cruelty among her own kith and kin.

This is a war not only to keep her family together but also to keep them decent.

Baba jan, there is a horrendous incident in the novel in which the Israeli soldiers in Ofer's platoon leave an old Palestinian man from the village of Dura in a meat locker for forty-eight hours. They had forgotten he was in the meat locker, and when they finally remembered and set him free, he had gone crazy. Ora cannot let go of the fact that Ofer had forgotten to release him. Her sympathies, her imagination, are with the Palestinian; she feels that "perhaps going out of his mind was the only way a Palestinian could get through all the checkpoints and the permits and the physical examination."

Ora's family will ultimately fall apart because she cannot accept the idea that her son has to kill someone, even if that someone is his enemy. In her state of rage and panic, she blames her country for intruding so violently upon her family's private life. "She felt the same old story again: this country, with its iron boot, had once again landed a thundering foot in a place where the state should not be." As the story progresses, we realize that its focus is on the unraveling of Ora's family life by a stronger external force, and her putting that life back together, making sense of it, through telling her story.

Ora is frightened that she will literally lose Ofer to war, but she is also frightened that she will lose him even if he survives but loses his essential humanity, or if that humanity comes to seem trivial to him in comparison to the urgency of the war. This is why she insists her son refrain from killing, even the enemy. She believes "that Ofer could not hurt a human being, because if that happened, even if there were a thousand justifications, even if the guy was about to detonate an explosive device, Ofer's life would never be the same. That was it. Quite simply, and irrefutably, he would have no life after that."

UNDER SUCH CIRCUMSTANCES, BABA JAN, how do you survive? And beyond just surviving, how do you lead your life decently, according to your principles? Grossman chooses what he calls the "literary approach." The way I understand this term is that literature is an act of resistance against dehumanization. War and trauma numb our senses and freeze our feelings. Literature restores us, awakens our feelings, and returns to us our sense of individuality and integrity. Both writing and reading become ways of protest; an existential rebellion against enforced violence. To remain human—or, more precisely, to remain *humane*—becomes the goal. We see this especially in the words and actions of Ora and Avram, the two storytellers in the novel. Ora turns to the magic of storytelling: through telling Ofer's story, she will save him from dying. As in *One Thousand and One Nights*, one story leads to another, and Ora connects Ofer's life to the stories of others during her walk with Avram. These stories are acts of resistance against death and oblivion.

As Ora's and Avram's journey progresses, we notice that, as in Scheherazade's story, both the teller and the listener are participating in the plot, becoming part of the tale. Avram, who had given up on life, gradually regains his senses through Ora's stories, and he realizes more fully the half-life he has been living since his time spent in enemy captivity. He is not King Shahryar, but like that king, through listening to Ora's stories, something slowly blooms in him. She evokes his previous life when he was so wildly alive, joyously brimming with words, when living and writing were so interwoven.

At the novel's end, we don't know what the future holds or whether Ofer will live or die. But we do know that something significant has taken place through the act of storytelling. And we know that, in a sense, Ora has taken back control from the state by becoming mistress of her own tale. No matter what happens, there is a place in her stories where Ofer will now live, and no one can take that life away from him. Once upon a time, desperate and in love, Ora and Avram conceived and gave birth to Ofer, and now "One day, not now, one day," Ora tells Avram, "you will write about our walk. . . . And in the end you'll see we'll give birth to a book."

DEAR BABA, DO YOU REMEMBER that gorgeous spring day in Tehran when you dropped by, as you often did, to take me and the children to the park? You might have forgotten it, but I doubt that. I want to go over it with you one more time, I don't ever want to forget it. I held Dara's hand, and you held Negar's. The day was tranquil, creating a false sense of calm and security. You were playing a game with the children that involved imaginary creatures who lived in the trees. You and the children talked about how the tree trunks and branches contained tunnels that led to the tree peoples' homes, and the roots connected the trees to one another and to an underground world beneath the trees. Then suddenly a cloud appeared in the distant sky, then the heavy sound of a rocket, then the smoke You and I froze and looked at each other. Negar and Dara kept shaking you, wanting you to go on with the story. And you acted as if the cloud was just a cloud and went on with it.

Do you remember that later that day, you told me that as long as we feel fear, we are alive? Our fears belong to life, are evidence that we are living, because the realm of death knows no fear. Except that you have to know how to control and resist your fears. You said you were sorry you had brought us up thinking we should never show our grief or fear. You said you should have taught us to feel fear and pain and to face up to them.

I so well remember that day, which had been so perfect before the rocket fell. I wanted to hold those moments, to make everything stop and return to the time before the rocket, before the jolt. No matter how many rockets hit the city, each always seemed as if it were the first. I just wanted the moment to freeze: you holding Negar's hand, me gripping Dara's, your voice low and mysterious as you described the tree people and their homes. But I do not believe in perfect days anymore, not since I have experienced the horror lodged deep in beauty and tenderness.

So, I want to freeze through writing that long-ago day we went to the park—the four of us: you, me, Negar, and Dara. We could have died, but we lived, and from then on, no tree was just a tree.

FOR BOTH KHOURY AND GROSSMAN, the act of storytelling is an act of love. There is always something hopeful and loving in the act of writing. Writing requires empathy, opening up oneself to other people's hearts and minds. It implies not just how things are but how they could be, which is the essence of hope.

Khoury goes into detail about Palestinian suffering, and yet he never seeks revenge. Instead, he turns to love. Believing

in the healing power of love, the author turns his story into
an amazing, poignant love story between Yunes and his wife,
Nahila. Yunes spends most of his time fighting, but he leads
another, much different life as well: he has turned a cave into
a secret meeting place with Nahila, where they make love, eat,
argue, exchange news, and which Yunes calls the Gate of Sun.

At one point, Khalil remembers that the novelist Kanafani
interviewed Yunes but decided not to write about him because
"he was looking for mythic stories, and yours was just the
story of a man in love. Where would be the symbolism in this
love that had no place to root itself? How did you expect he
would believe the story of your love for your wife? Is a man's
love for his wife really worth writing about?" How would you
answer this question, dear Baba?

As the story unfolds, we realize Yunes the fighter would
have been an empty shell—his life or death meaningless—
had he not loved Nahila with ferocity and tenderness. You
would not expect this, Baba jan, from a fighter with a cause,
but as we ourselves discovered during a war and a revolution,
it is amazing how much love matters under such extreme
conditions. When atrocities happen that make you lose your
faith in humanity, and in your own sense of being human,
that faith is restored by the love of one individual. Khalil asks
Yunes, "Every time, you purchased your love at the cost of the
possibility of your death. Isn't that extraordinary? Isn't that
story like no other?"

AS I NEAR THE END of this letter, I feel lighter, but I am still
not sure I have effectively expressed the sense of both joy
and anguish that accompanied me while reading *To the End*

of the Land, nor the tenderness and grief I felt when reading *Gate of the Sun*, nor the sense of connection and humanity I experienced reading *Places and Names*. Nor am I sure that my arguments would have satisfied that young man so taken by facts. None of the works I have discussed with you in this letter are the kind that warm the cockles of your heart, making you all fuzzy and comfortable. They are not soothing, but disturbing—all the more so because they get to the core of the facts, making us see them and see beyond them. Facts, like that proverbial clay, need to be shaped and breathed into in order to become alive, and they *do* come alive in these books. Just as you made stories come alive and made us all richer for it.

As I write these words, I remember Avram whispering to Ora, "Though I walk through the valley of the shadow of death, I will fear no evil, for my story is with me."

> With love
> Baba's daughter,
> Azi

ATWOOD

MAY 11–26, 2020

Dearest Baba,

This morning I woke up around five, earlier than usual, and since I couldn't get back to sleep, I got up, made myself some coffee, and took my cup to the balcony to salute the Potomac. It was still dark, and I could feel the river rather than see it. I was experiencing two kinds of silence simultaneously. One was the silence of the river at early morning, its beauty and calm, the trees shadowlike in the darkness. Then there was the other, inner silence; the feeling I get whenever I think of the virus, disturbing and insidious. There is a silence to the coronavirus, like that of death, as if the dread of the virus wraps itself around me like mist. This silence is charged with menace, of the kind that won't go away with tranquilizers. It is more existential. Unlike during the Iran-Iraq War, the threat does not come with loud noises, but follows me, encircles me, cold and clammy.

Then there is the silence of the book I write to you about today, Baba, Margaret Atwood's *The Handmaid's Tale*. It occurs to me that in *The Handmaid's Tale*, the author creates these two kinds of silence side by side: beauty and death, the kind you and I experienced, living in a totalitarian society, feeling the danger in the air even in moments of relative peace and calm.

I had always wanted to talk to Margaret Atwood about *The Handmaid's Tale*. Before her book became a runaway success and was made into a popular television series, it seemed as if the American people had instinctively associated Trump's mindset with that of the rulers in Atwood's Gilead. When I first met her at the Toronto International Festival of Authors, held at the Harbour Front Center, where we spoke briefly, she told me that her books had been translated into Persian. At the time, I thought of telling her about my experience of first reading *The Handmaid's Tale*—about how difficult it was for me to read, about how it blurred the boundaries between her fiction and my reality, collapsing one into the other so that, at first, I reacted to her fiction as if it *were* my reality. But I didn't tell her any of these things back then; there simply was not enough time for me to explain myself.

Now there has been a surge of interest in *The Handmaid's Tale*, and in its 2019 sequel, *The Testaments*, in my adopted home country, America. Though I no longer live in Iran, reality in Trump's America is becoming more and more not just unreal or surreal, but *irreal*, tinged with anxiety about where this country is headed. You, Baba jan, might tell me that this America is not that Islamic Republic. And you are right, but there are also signs and manifestations of a totalitarian mindset in Trump and his supporters that shouldn't be underestimated.

Now that *The Handmaid's Tale* has become a bestseller again in America, I became curious to know how it had fared

in Iran. So I called Shirin, an ardent reader. She said our
common friend Maryam, a prominent translator, had told her
that many of Atwood's books had been translated and that
The Handmaid's Tale was very popular, having gone through
eleven printings. "But I don't know how I read it," she said.
"The book was unbearable. The world in Atwood's book,
I have been living it for the past forty years, and I have no
intention of living it twice."

Shirin said the worst thing about it, from what she heard
from me and other friends in the US, was that so many
Americans felt the totalitarian Republic of Gilead in Atwood's
book was a terrible place, to be avoided at all costs in America,
but that something similar to it, like the Islamic Republic, was
good for us in Iran because it represented "our culture." Worse
than that, I replied, is the fact that the American republic
might go the way of the Republic of Gilead. After all, I said,
Atwood has placed her Gilead in the former United States of
America. From there, we digressed to talk about one of our
favorite topics: how the Islamic Republic, in order to justify its
rule, claimed that the theocracy it had imposed on our people
was based on Iran's true culture and traditions.

I told Shirin how difficult it was for me to see this fake
claim accepted by so many on both the Right and the Left
in the West, especially in America. How condescending to
believe that others from other cultures don't want to be as
free as we are, and that their women do not wish for the same
rights American women fought for— this, despite the fact
that women in most of these cultures, including Iran, have,
for more than a century, fought and are fighting for those
very rights that women in the West demand. So many times
when I have lamented the plight of women under the Islamic

Republic, I have heard, "But you are being Western" and "It's their culture!"

Shirin agreed, saying, "We have thousands of years of history and culture. Most of our history, when we were the greatest empire in the ancient world, is pre-Islamic anyway! And we also produced so many great poets, scientists, and philosophers during the Islamic period. We know so much about Western history and culture. What does the West know about our history and culture? What do its people know about our poets, scientists, and philosophers?"

I remember, Baba jan, you always complained about how little the American people, even their policy makers and public figures, knew about other countries. For you, they wore their ignorance good naturedly and casually. The world, you felt, knew much about America, but America knew little about the world. You would not be surprised by this utter ignorance about Iran and the rest of the countries of the "Muslim world."

I told Shirin that when I'd returned to US in 1997, I was already noticing a shift in the attitude toward these countries. This, of course, only became more pronounced and more accepted after September 11. To my utter surprise and dismay, the myth that the Islamic Republic had created about Iran and Islam had been accepted and extended to all Muslim-majority countries. All these nations, with vastly different histories, nationalities, languages, and cultures were reduced into one aspect: religion. And that religion, which, like other religions, had many different denominations and interpretations, was brought down to its most extreme elements: fundamentalism and Sharia law. So now these countries were even deprived of their proper names and were all generalized into the Muslim world, denying the diversity of Islam and its followers. It's like saying that France, Britain, and the United States are all Christian countries and part of the "Christian world"!

Those on the far Right, like Trump, use this argument for reactionary and racist policies against those from Muslim-majority countries with the excuse that brutality is "their culture," while on the far Left, some have decided that since this is "their culture," we should not criticize "them," refusing to differentiate between the rulers and the ruled, the regimes that created such mythologies and the people upon whom they are imposed. It is like saying Trump's America is the whole of America, I said to Shirin.

We chatted for a while longer, and by the time we hung up, the sky had brightened, the surface of the Potomac gleaming with small waves. The high-rise buildings on the other side of the river in Virginia had begun appearing behind the trees, and I was drinking my third cup of coffee. I remembered that Mitra, another friend, and, like me, an immigrant, also told me it was difficult for her to read *The Handmaid's Tale*. "It got too much under my skin," she said. My friends were avid readers and had little difficulty reading heart-wrenching dystopian novels such as *1984*. What had made Atwood's book so difficult for them to read?

I FIRST READ *THE HANDMAID'S TALE* in 1998. The story takes place in a theocracy after the US government has been overthrown. It is narrated by a woman called Offred, one of the "Handmaids" whose task is to bear children for the male ruling elite, called the "Commanders." At the time of reading the book, my memories of life in the Islamic Republic were still raw—I might have physically been living in the US, but emotionally I was still very much in Iran. Especially at night; I had nightmares and felt claustrophobic.

In those first years following my return from Iran, I read a great deal, making up for all the books I had not been allowed to read there. I moved from one author to the next, trying to read all of their books. I devoured Atwood's books one after another: *Alias Grace, Wilderness Tips, Surfacing, Lady Oracle, The Edible Woman*. As I read the first chapters of *The Handmaid's Tale*, I was struck by the similarities between her book's theocratic Republic of Gilead and the Islamic Republic of Iran—it stirred up many familiar feelings and emotions for me.

Baba jan, the similarities between the book and the Islamic Republic are not just my conjectures. *The Handmaid's Tale* ends with an academic conference set in the future. The main speaker, an expert on the Republic of Gilead, Professor Pieixoto, has written a paper titled "Iran and Gilead: Two Late-Twentieth-Century Monotheocracies, as Seen Through Diaries." Clearly, Atwood was aware of the similarities between Gilead and the Islamic Republic of Iran. But more pertinently, if we find that this book mirrors our reality, it is because Atwood has so brilliantly used historical fact to inform her fiction. Baba, I bet if you had read the story, you would have agreed with me that apart from the similarities in details, Atwood has captured the atmosphere and the mood of a totalitarian society like the Islamic Republic.

In 2017 Atwood wrote an essay for the *New York Times* on the meaning of *The Handmaid's Tale* in the age of Trump, in which she confirms that all the events in the book are based on facts. Some of these facts were gathered during her visits to Eastern Europe during the Soviet era. Alluding to a line from a poem by the American poet Marianne Moore, she explains this decision: "If I was to create an imaginary garden, I wanted the toads in it to be real." For those of us who had experienced the Islamic Republic, her toads were only too real. In this piece, she also reveals, "One of my rules was that I would not put any events into the book that had not already happened in what James Joyce called the 'nightmare of history.'"

Though her *Times* piece states that the novel's facts were based on real events in the West, they created an imaginary theocratic republic that was the fictional sibling of the Islamic Republic of Iran. In her article, Atwood mentions that the Republic of Gilead, formed after a coup in the United States, is "built on a foundation of the seventeenth-century Puritan roots that have always lain beneath the modern-day America we thought we knew," down to the modest clothing Atwood's women wear. She adds, "So many strands fed into *The Handmaid's Tale*: group executions, sumptuary laws, book burnings, the Lebensborn program of the SS [initiated by the SS and supported by the state, aimed at raising the birth rate of Aryan children born of parents who were "racially pure"] and the child stealing of the Argentine generals, the history of slavery, the history of American polygamy . . ."

Baba jan, you might be unconvinced by my argument, so let me tell you about the ways that the Republic of Gilead mirrored the Islamic Republic of Iran. To begin, Gilead, like Iran, is a theocracy—or what Atwood calls a monotheocracy, where citizens are governed by divine rule and controlled through extreme fear and violence. The public hangings in Gilead are like the public hangings and stoning we witnessed in Iran. In Gilead, we see persecution of religious minorities and Christian denominations such as Baptists, Catholics, and Quakers, whose views differ from the extreme religious beliefs of the rulers of Gilead. This is similar to the way the Islamic Republic oppresses not only Jews, Baha'is, Zoroastrians, Christians, and atheists, but also Muslim sects such as the Sunnis, Sufis, and Shaykhis. Both republics persecute women and minorities. Both regard women as feebleminded, subservient to men, their bodies sinful, requiring coverage from head to foot. I guess we have to thank our lucky stars that in some ways things are not quite as bad for women in Iran as for their counterparts in Gilead, where women are prohibited from reading and writing and are classified according to a dehumanizing hierarchy. In Iran, there is censorship and banning of books, but there are no distinctions made between men and women in this regard.

In Gilead, wives of the elite Commanders are at the top of the food chain, above "Marthas," who are similar to domestic servants, and "Econowives," who belong to the lowest classes. Handmaids seem to be in a class of their own; they are deemed important, but only as breeding machines. I feel a great deal for the Handmaids and their plight. We could see why, in a country such as Gilead, high infertility rates would cause concern, but the regime's solution to this problem is brutal. The idea that these young, fertile women are forced into a bizarre monthly ritual of copulating with the Commander assigned to them, and that any child they gave birth to belongs not to them but to the Commander's wife, is horrifying. Not only that, but if a Handmaid turns out to be infertile, her fate is a certain death or banishment to colonies that could be worse than death.

In Gilead, women known as "Aunts" do not marry, and they are the only women who are allowed to read and write because their task is to brainwash and indoctrinate other women. Now that I think about it, the Aunts in Gilead are in some ways similar to certain women in the Islamic Republic, who, along with armed men, patrolled the streets of our cities, looking for the badly Hijabed women, arresting them, preaching to them, trying to force them to repent their sinful ways and to follow God's edicts—while escorting them to jail. You remember them, Baba? They were the morality squads calling themselves Blood of God. But Iranian women resisted and wouldn't relent: even after being arrested and punished, once out of jail, they'd go back to repeating the same "offense." Finally, the regime decided the patrols were not effective and stopped them. In the same manner, women's resistance led to many other retreats by the regime regarding women's public appearances; the laws have not changed, but they have become increasingly difficult to implement.

BABA JAN, BOTH COUNTRIES I have called home have become so absurd in recent months that at times I feel as if I am in a psychedelic song by one of my favorite bands, Queen, as if I too, like Freddie Mercury, am going slightly mad. My friend Shirin told me to read Ayatollah Khamenei, the supreme leader of the Islamic Republic's message on March 21 on the occasion of the Iranian new year. Khamenei mentioned the coronavirus in his speech—not to organize a reasoned response to the virus, but to claim that the supernatural creatures known as genies were plotting with human enemies against the Islamic Republic. He said, "We have both the genie and human enemies that help one another. The intelligence services of many countries work together against us." Refusing medical help from both America and Doctors Without Borders, he said that the "most evil enemy of the Islamic Republic"—namely, America— has created a medicine that is seemingly for treatment but may even entrench the disease in Iran rather than eradicate it. Drawing parallels between himself and the Prophet, Khamenei believes that the US has developed a strain of the virus that will affect only the Iranians.

I told Shirin that superstition and conspiracy theories are also abundant in the United States, where we have Trump, who is in the habit of drawing parallels between himself and great historical figures such as Abraham Lincoln, and who has claimed, among other things, that to cure COVID-19 we should inject ourselves with bleach. These leaders are claiming such absurdities while their people are dying from the virus every day. Let us not forget that in the very early days of the pandemic, Iran had one of the worst infection rates and death rates in the world. The Iranian government has given up on protecting the population even at the most elementary level. Instead, it pours its efforts into controlling the information about the number of casualties and threatening medical staff to remain quiet. Trump, meanwhile, blunders on in denial. Nowadays, whether in the Islamic Republic or the United States of America, a lot happens that belongs to the absurd. The tragedy is that we are living this absurdity and somehow tolerating it.

IN HER *NEW YORK TIMES* PIECE, Atwood mentions that the precedent for the ritual imposed on the Handmaids can be found in the biblical story of Jacob, his two wives, Rachel and Leah, and their maids. Rachel, who is "barren," tells Jacob to sleep with her maid Bilhah to provide her with children: "Behold my maid Bilhah, go in unto her; and she shall bear upon my knees, that I may also have children by her." So, Baba jan, in addition to having no control over their own bodies or their children, the Handmaids are not even allowed to keep their own names. They are instead referred to by the prefix "Of," followed by the first name of their Commander. The protagonist in *The Handmaid's Tale*, for example, is called Offred. Of Fred.

Okay, the Islamic Republic does not have Handmaids, but in both Gilead and Iran, women's bodies are deemed transgressive, made for procreation and to be at the service of men. As in Gilead, women in Iran are told to beware of men's gazes. Women must make themselves invisible to men because their bodies are sources of sin and temptation, which is why, in both societies, women's bodies and hair should be covered. As Atwood writes: "Modesty is invisibility, said Aunt Lydia. Never forget it. To be seen—to be *seen*—is to be—her voice trembled—penetrated."

Baba jan, I constantly have to explain to so many people over here that if today in Iran the issue of the mandatory veil has become so central to Iranian women's struggles, it is because their public appearance has become the symbol of the state's power and control over the populace. So, here in America, I keep explaining to whoever is interested that the mandatory veil forced on Iranian women after the 1979 revolution had little to do with faith and everything to do with state's control of its citizens through imposing uniformity, making women invisible and depriving them of power. And the fight against the mandatory veil is not a fight against religion, but for freedom of choice and expression, which is why some women who voluntarily wear the veil support the fight against it. I am reminded of what Offred says about her body: "I avoid looking down at my body, not so much because it is shameful or immodest but because I don't want to see it. I don't want to look at something that determines me so completely."

Baba jan, do you see how in both republics, religion is turned into ideology, into an instrument of power, and religion itself has become a casualty of that power? You know as well as I that the laws against women, instituted after the revolution, were based on the misogynist viewpoint that women are intellectually inferior to men. You, Baba jan, hated it as much as I did that female judges in Iran were defrocked, and that in court, women's testimony counts only as half of men's. We were outraged by the way the new regime replaced all the progressive laws regarding women with the Sharia laws, which mandate, for example, that when Iranian couples divorce, child custody should always be awarded to the father—and, in the event of the father's death, it must go to his nearest male family member. I still feel sick when I think how they legitimized polygamy and temporary marriages for men, but women are stoned to death for what they called adultery and prostitution. These are the laws, dear Baba, that the apologists for the regime call "our culture"!

You remember how angry we were when, at the start of the revolution, the regime changed the age of marriage for females from eighteen to nine? My God, it was only after Iranian women activists' protests and struggles to change the law that the regime finally raised it to thirteen (thirteen!), although girls under that age can be married with the consent of their fathers and a religious judge.

In both Iran and in Gilead, what is being denied is a woman's autonomy, her individuality, and the right to choose a path for her own life. Baba jan, I am amazed at how even small details of life in Gilead mirror life in the Islamic Republic. For example, in Iran, the regime compares women to pearls in an oyster, pearls being symbols of modesty and chastity. The same concept is applied to women in Gilead. In Gilead as in the Islamic Republic of Iran, images of women where any exposed part of the body, other than their face and hands, are painted over.

But it is not merely these details that make the two republics siblings. What is most striking is the verisimilitude of this novel. The Gilead that Atwood has managed to create is so very real in the sense that it has the same claustrophobic, fear-ridden atmosphere as the Islamic Republic—the same kind of mindset rules over both.

Dear Baba, I am grateful to you for insisting that we talk to our children about Iran's true history and culture. They would not get that knowledge from the schools, you said, so it would be up to us to educate them. And you were right. In every totalitarian society, confiscating and reshaping the citizens' reality begins with confiscating and rewriting history. To justify the present, the past must be obliterated and reinvented. In Gilead, as in the Islamic Republic, before the revolution, women had many rights and were active in all walks of life. Offred worked; Aunt Lydia was a judge. Baba jan, until the revolution, I had taken the amazing achievements of the Iranian women for granted. I have talked about it often with Shirin. We recalled how it all seemed so natural to so many of us that women should participate in all walks of life; that alongside female engineers and pilots would be female judges, members of the parliament (my own mother being among the first six women admitted to the National Iranian Congress), as well as government ministers—including a minister for women's affairs, only the second woman in the world to hold this position.

It is because of this history of women's struggles for their rights and their achievements that they could stand up to the Islamic regime and refuse to give up their hard-earned rights. All this seemed natural to us, as if it had always been that way, as if for generations—even before my grandmother's time—women had not fought for their rights, as if these rights that had been won through so much sacrifice and suffering were forever ours and could never be taken away from us. I remember wondering how we could not see that the rights we enjoyed had been the result of long years of fighting by our mothers, grandmothers, and even great-grandmothers. Shirin felt that this was a generational thing. She said it seems as if each new generation born into the comfort and privileges gained by the hard struggles of previous generations take those comforts and privileges for granted, never having had to work for them. As in Gilead, now most of this is gone; even the right to dress the way we want, the way we used to dress, is now, as Offred says, banned and being called "Westernized."

OKAY, BABA JAN, SO WE have proven that Margaret Atwood's Gilead has a lot in common with our Islamic Republic. But really, so what? The way I see it, some women read *The Handmaid's Tale* because they identify with it, and some cannot read it for the same reason; but neither should be the reason we read a book. You see, the similarities between our reality and Atwood's fiction do not explain my fascination with her novel or why I felt so invested in the fate of each character. In a paradoxical way, reading her book both brings me back to life in the Islamic Republic and lifts me out of it and into the world of the story. The fact of my personal experience should and does add another dimension to my reading of the book. I do understand and empathize with Shirin and her difficulty reading Atwood's novel while living in the present-day Iran—we cannot simply ignore the realities of people's lives. But I refuse to allow the Islamic Republic to monopolize my thoughts and feelings to such an extent that I cannot read a work of fiction as a separate entity from my reality.

LATER TODAY, AFTER MY FOURTH cup of coffee, as I continued to struggle with this letter to you, some inarticulate sense of excitement kept me pacing from one end of the room to another, pausing by the living room window to watch a lone boat on the river, two joggers on the sidewalk, and the cars silently on the move.

I turned away and called Shirin in Iran again. After a hasty greeting, I blurted out: "What is fascinating about Atwood's book is not its resemblance to the Islamic Republic, but how universal these things are!"

"What things?" asked Shirin.

"Totalitarianism and democracy," I replied. Just think about it: Is it accidental that Atwood, rather than choosing an imaginary place for her story, or an actual authoritarian society, chooses to place Gilead in the United States of America? This implies, I told Shirin, that totalitarianism and democracy are not limited to one specific country or nation. I mentioned to her what Atwood says in her *New York Times* piece about the fact that all the events in *The Handmaid's Tale*, including the women covering their bodies and hair, were based on things that had already happened in the West. More proof, I said, that the cultural determinism in Iran that we both so resented and deplored was wrong; that no matter where you live, West or East, there exist both regressive and progressive traditions.

"We can preserve the best and get rid of the worst!" I told my friend triumphantly. I spoke breathlessly, as though if I didn't tell her these things right there and then, the ideas would be lost forever. "The fight for freedom of choice and association among other freedoms is not a western tradition, but a human need," I went on to say. Then I read Shirin a quote from Frederick Douglass that I had written on a page at the end of Atwood's book: "A smile or a tear has not nationality; joy and sorrow speak alike to all nations, and they, above all the confusion of tongues, proclaim the brotherhood of man."

BABA JAN, I FEEL GREAT anxiety about Negar's and Kelli's pregnancies, something I am trying very hard to refrain from telling them. I don't want to burden them with my worries, but I distinctly remember the experience of being pregnant with both Negar and later Dara during the war. In addition to my general fears and anxieties, I kept hearing about how children born in wartime were sometimes born with birth defects because their mothers lived in a constant state of tension and stress. So, in addition to the actual tension I felt about the war, I carried the burden of worrying about my unborn babies, especially Dara, with whom I was pregnant during some nasty attacks on Tehran. I now have the same anxieties about my grandchildren being born during a different war: a pandemic. I wonder if Kelli and Negar also feel the same fears, but I don't want to ask them. I keep reminding myself that despite my anxieties, both my children were born healthy, but that in itself is not enough to quiet my concerns.

HAVE YOU THOUGHT ABOUT THE role that ordinary, often decent, people play in bringing about a totalitarian state? Such systems may seem to appear out of nowhere, like a bolt of lightning. But really, this is because many choose not to see the warning signs, even when they become all too obvious. Slowly, over time, there is a buildup. At first, the rulers may target people and things that are unsavory to us, and that we dislike or disapprove of—as they did in Iran, when they executed officials of the former regime. So we shrug them off, or we might even approve, but our time will come when they take away what pleases us, what is important to us. It is like the reaction to the virus, when people hope things will get better, but they won't until we do something about it.

Around the beginning of the theocratic revolution, Offred realizes gradually that indifference toward the suppression of others, even those we disagree with and disapprove of, could one day lead to her own suppression. "Things continued in that state of suspended animation for weeks," she tells us, "although some things did happen. Newspapers were censored, and some were closed down—for security reasons, they said. The roadblocks began to appear, and Identipasses. Everyone approved of that, since it was obvious you couldn't be too careful. They said that new elections would be held but that it would take some time to prepare for them. The thing to do, they said, was to continue on as usual." And they continued as usual in those unusual times. People didn't do anything to strike back at the new regime. They stopped protest marches in the streets for fear of being shot at. Soon they *couldn't* do anything. Doesn't all this remind you of Iran at the beginning of the Islamic Revolution?

In *The Testaments*, Atwood's sequel, Aunt Lydia remembers that long before the new regime took power, "things had been on a downward spiral for years." At first, people became frightened, then angry, and, in the "absence of viable remedies," they looked for someone to blame. "Why did I think it would nonetheless be business as usual?" she asks. "Because we'd been hearing these things for so long, I suppose you don't believe the sky is falling until a chunk of it falls on you." Dear Baba, I have seen the same thing happen in America, which is by no means a totalitarian state, and where we can still freely voice our protest and our opposition. Still, I have witnessed the actions of a government that violates the most fundamental values and principles of this country, kowtowing to hostile foreign powers and endangering the country's national security. Leaders who routinely lie, commit crimes, and perpetrate cover-ups. And yet a sizable number of people still believe "it" (totalitarianism) can't happen here,

standing behind Trump, shouting, "Make America Great
Again!"

NOW IT'S LATE AFTERNOON, and I am up to my fifth cup of
coffee. This time I pour a little brandy in it. I need something
different, something to calm me down, though I don't think
coffee with brandy is the answer. The view from my balcony
is so beautiful; I wish you were here to see it, Baba. It rained
earlier, and then the light began to seep through the new
green leaves. Clouds had covered the sky, but now a pale sun
illuminated the river, the trees, and the buildings on the other
side of the river. It stayed this way for a very short while, and
then the sun truly asserted itself.

Back to our story. Baba jan. At some point in the book,
Offred says, "I believe in resistance, as I believe there can be
no light without shadow; or, rather, no shadow unless there
is also light." I agree with her. I believe in that light. I have
witnessed it. How to resist? When we think of totalitarian
systems, we think of the extremes, of torture, of executions,
of barbaric behavior. In Gilead, there are public hangings
where the bodies of victims remain on display for days for
all to see. These are hysterical murders in which masses
participate, not so unlike the public hangings, stonings,
tortures, and rapes of the Islamic Republic. These are crimes
of spectacle, designed to instill fear and paralysis in citizens'
hearts and spirit. I have seen pictures of Iranian children
watching these public executions alongside the adults. What
is extraordinary, what is incredible and shocking, becomes
ordinary, routine, even mundane. As Aunt Lydia puts it in *The
Testaments*, "Ordinary . . . is what you are used to. This may

not seem ordinary to you now, but after a time it will. It will become ordinary."

Baba, this is what I fear most: that things once considered horrific should become ordinary, that people should get used to even extreme violence and learn to live with it. The first step in resisting totalitarianism is refusing to allow extreme brutalities or the confiscation of individual freedoms to become routine or ordinary. Offred instinctively resists— she finds ways to remind herself that she does not belong in this system, even refusing to call the room where she stays in her Commander's house "my room." She is forced to witness the brutalities but never becomes a part of them, never becomes used to them. One's first impulse in the face of such brutalities is to close the eyes, to turn away, to try and forget. But the point is that we must never let these atrocities become ordinary or accepted.

In Iran, my first impulse was to ignore the news, ignore the very reality around and about me, or try to normalize it, accept it, and get on with my life. I would avoid watching the news or reading the papers, I would shut myself in my room and read for long stretches of time, but none of this worked. It was such a difficult task, when I tried not to get used to things, not to evade them: the officials' harangues on television, the show trials, pictures of those executed, the stories about executions, and flogging for possession of alcoholic beverages and music cassettes, the nightly roadblocks, the accounts of torture.

DEAR BABA, HAVE YOU NOTICED that when extraordinary events become part of everyday life in a totalitarian society, what used to be routine, normal, taken for granted, becomes extraordinary, rare, out of reach? The fact is that the rulers in Gilead ruled not just by extreme violence but also by taking away what we consider small freedoms—so seemingly small that while we have them, we take them for granted, consider them our birthrights, don't even regard them as freedoms, fought for and fragile.

It has been said that totalitarianism is in essence against life, so living in itself, enjoying the very act of being alive, becomes an act of transgression. Totalitarian systems are against pleasure, against joy or beauty; there is a self-righteous puritanism to them that turns simple pleasures into sinful temptations. "But a chair, sunlight, flowers: these are not to be dismissed." So says Offred, adding, "I am alive, live, I breathe, I put my hand out, unfolded, into the sunlight. Where I am is not a prison, but a privilege, as Aunt Lydia said, who was in love with either/or."

In real life, Eugenia Ginzburg, imprisoned for eighteen years in one of the Soviet Union's Siberian gulags under brutal dictator Joseph Stalin, wrote: "I felt instinctively that as long as I could be stirred to emotion by the sea breeze, by the brilliance of the stars, and by poetry, I would still be alive, however much my legs might tremble and my back bend under the load of burning stones." Often, Offred thinks of her past: her lover and later husband, Luke; their daughter; the simple freedoms she took for granted. "We thought we had such problems," she says. "How were we to know we were happy?" When Offred runs into a group of Japanese tourists dressed the way she used to before Gilead, she remarks wistfully, "I used to dress like that. That was freedom. *Westernized*, they used to call it."

In Iran, as in Gilead, these pleasures and privileges are called Western and are wrested away from the citizens. In America today, these rights could fade and may one day perish because of indifference, because we don't understand they are not simply our birth rights, but our privilege. We sometimes forget that once upon a time in this country human beings were bought and sold as chattel, that there were restrictions on how women could appear and act in both public and private, that they did not have the right to vote, that they could not enter many institutions of higher learning, that they did not have control over their property, that very few jobs were open to them, and that all this was accepted by a large segment of the society as American culture—yes, here in America.

In Gilead and in Iran, it is obvious that ordinary citizens, especially women, are the victims, the constant targets of totalitarian regimes. What is not so obvious is the power that the people, especially women, hold over the system. The most targeted, the most victimized are also the most dangerous, the most deadly. Just the fact that women have to cover their bodies gives them power over the men, even men (and at times especially men) like Offred's Commander, who crave what they themselves have forbidden. The very fact that they restrict women, try to keep them subservient and cover them up, indicates how afraid they are of the power of women. Even in a democracy, Trump and his followers' hatred and disdain for immigrants, minorities, women, show their fear: "What if 'these people' replace me?"

As you know well, Iranian women sensed their power from the very start. Many never complied with the laws regarding the mandatory veil or the way they appeared in public. They would go to jail for it, be flogged and reappear in the same subversive manner. It was much easier for the regime to jail and destroy political groups and organizations than to force millions of women to comply, to submit. You wouldn't know this, but the refusal to collaborate with the regime in recent years has turned into a movement.

A lot has happened since you were gone. Masih Alinejad, a young woman, born in an Iranian village in a conservative, and religious family, had gradually become so disenchanted with the theocratic system that she migrated first to Britain and then to America. She created a website called Iranian Women's Stealthy Freedoms and posted photos of women without their Hijab. Soon this act turned into a movement: men in solidarity with women wore veils while women took theirs off, veiled women took photos with unveiled ones. I liked their hashtag: #OurCameraIsOurWeapon. The regime, with all its guns, did not have the power to suppress the women with their cameras. You won't believe that right now, as I write this letter, how many women activists are in jail, having been sentenced to long years of imprisonment mainly because of their protest against the mandatory veil.

BABA JAN, YOU MUST INDULGE me in making the following outlandish claim: Would you believe that I have found some common themes between *The Handmaid's Tale* and Jane Austen's *Pride and Prejudice?* Both novels, as with so many great works of literature that feature women protagonists, are about freedom of choice, and they are in essence celebrations of ordinary life. *The Handmaid's Tale*, like any great novel, is also a celebration of life, of falling in love, buying clothes, having your own money in your own name at the bank, owning a cat. As with *Pride and Prejudice*, it is about women's search for independence and freedom of choice. What surprised me while reading *The Handmaid's Tale* was not the extreme violence, but this celebration of ordinary life, as well as its subversive nature: Offred hoarding butter and margarine from her food tray to use as cream to keep her skin soft, her desire to be touched by another human being, her small moves to tease the men in power, and risking her life to make love to the one man she has found desirable during her time in Gilead.

I love the scene where she is saluted by guards, called "Guardians"; curious, one of them tries to look at her face, and she raises her head a little to facilitate this. She says to the reader, "It's an event, a small defiance of rule, so small as to be undetectable, but such moments are the rewards I hold out for myself, like the candy I hoarded, as a child, at the back of a drawer. Such moments are possibilities, tiny peepholes." Through such seemingly small acts, Offred attempts to keep vestiges of her confiscated identity and individuality, declaring a form of independence from the totalitarian power of Gilead.

I so get it, that urge toward small transgressions, like a child being naughty and eating the forbidden candy. Once, at the university where I worked in Tehran, I deliberately shook hands with a male colleague, which, at the time, was strictly forbidden. I could almost hear the drawing in of the breath by two other colleagues who witnessed this act of transgression, and I could see the effort it took my shocked male colleague, trying to be polite, as he resisted withdrawing his hand. Every so often, I would do something like this. To others, it may have seemed silly or reckless or even pointless—acting out wouldn't change anything. But these small acts of rebellion helped me to remember who I was. Similarly, I had a friend who, whenever she appeared in public with her boyfriend, itself already against the law, obstinately held hands with him. Just a gesture: you don't own me, you don't control my actions, my feelings, my thoughts.

Dear Baba, do you notice how, under totalitarianism, banal rituals like putting on body lotion or holding hands with a loved one in the street suddenly become strange and extraordinary? Ordinary people wanting to have a decent, normal life learn that nothing is normal—not really, we only carry the illusions of normalcy. If we don't pay attention, if we don't guard against this loss of normalcy, it is easy to lose. This is what we see Offred doing her best to guard against as she tries to avoid the numbing of feelings and emotions that a totalitarian system imposes on us.

I AM SURE I AM not wrong in thinking that one of the main questions at the heart of both *The Handmaid's Tale* and *The Testaments* is the dehumanization and obliteration of those who oppose you or are different from you. I have talked to you in a previous letter about the dehumanization of the enemy during wars, but in a totalitarian society, the "war" is against one's own citizens, who are divided into insiders if they obey and outsiders if they don't.

Offred describes an incident that illustrates the kind of dehumanization that can happen under totalitarianism: she and her husband decide to escape the newly formed revolutionary regime, but in order to do so they need to get rid of their cat. Luke tells Offred that he will take care of the problem. As Offred tells us: "I'll take care of it, Luke said. And because he had said *it* instead of *her*, I knew he meant *kill*. That is what you have to do before you kill, I thought. You have to create an *it* where none was before. You do that first, in your head, and then you make it real. So that's how they do it, I thought."

An interesting complication in *The Handmaid's Tale* is the developing relationship between Offred and her Commander. At first, they belong to opposing camps; neither is wholly human to the other. Offred is a fertility machine there to provide the Commander and his wife with a child, and the Commander to her is the oppressor who arbitrarily holds the right to her life and death. But then the Commander expresses a wish to see Offred in secret. And what he demands of her when they meet is not sex but something more bizarre: to play Scrabble and, upon parting, for her to kiss him as if she "meant it."

Gradually, their relationship develops over more secret meetings, and the Commander increasingly tries to act as if they live in the past, in pre-Gileadean times. "I remind myself," Offred says, "that he is not an unkind man—that under other circumstances, I even like him." The relationship has changed. Before, he seemed all powerful, but now she realizes she has bargaining power, that he wants something from her, and that gives her some power over him. "He was no longer a thing to me," Offred tells us. "That was the problem. I realized it that night, and the realization has stayed with me. It complicates."

Baba, similar "complications" arise in *The Testaments*. This novel has three narrators, or witnesses: Offred's older daughter, who was born before the rise of Gilead and was

taken away from her; Offred's younger daughter, who was
smuggled to Canada and has returned to Gilead on a secret
mission; and the infamous Aunt Lydia, who is, in my opinion,
the most interesting and complicated narrator. Lydia is the
Chief Aunt, in charge of women's indoctrination in Gilead,
and here the enemy has been given her own voice and her
own space in which to express her perspective. Before the
Gileadean revolution, Lydia was a judge. But like all other
working women, she was arrested, tortured, kept in solitary
confinement and humiliated, and then offered a choice:
either agree to become part of the system—to help build and
structure it—or else be executed.

She chooses the system. But there is a twist here. She
writes, "Did I weep? Yes: tears came out of my two visible
eyes, my moist weeping human eyes. But I had a third eye,
in the middle of my forehead. I could feel it: it was cold, like
a stone. It did not weep: it saw. And behind it someone was
thinking: I will get you back for this. I don't care how long
it takes or how much shit I have to eat in the meantime, but
I will do it." Aunt Lydia decides to join the Gilead elite, but
deep down, she is out to "get" them, to destroy Gilead.

Before I forget, Baba jan, I wanted to mention that one of
the most subversive turns in these two books is the way they
implicate all of us, while refusing to make compromises. We,
as readers, are 100 percent behind the victims—the women
of Gilead—but Atwood doesn't allow us to become simple
cheerleaders for them, for they too are human and fallible.
The fact that they are victims does not mean that they are
pure and incapable of evil. To this end, in her *New York Times*
piece, Atwood writes, "Yes, women will gang up on other
women. Yes, they will accuse others to keep themselves off

the hook: we see that very publicly in the age of social media, which enables group warnings. Yes, they will gladly take positions of power over other women, even—and possibly, especially—in systems in which women as a whole have scant power."

Like the Commander, Aunt Lydia complicates the issues and makes our judgment of her difficult. How do we define her? She is a victim, tortured and subjected to the worst kind of treatment. She is also a villain, one of the most powerful people in Gilead, having helped to create it, and give it structure. She is a savior, amassing evidence against Gilead, helping the resistance, causing its downfall. Who is Aunt Lydia? Baba jan, I am reminded of the incident when you were in jail, and the head of the dreaded secret police paid you a visit. During your conversation, he was so touched that he started crying. Here you were with one of the most powerful men in the country crying in front of you. That incident did not make him stop harassing you, nor did it make you justify his actions, but it showed you a different side of him. It humanized him.

BABA, SOMETIMES IT IS THROUGH extreme conditions that we realize the importance of imagination and ideas to our survival as human beings—extreme conditions reflect what our normal lives could become. I am reminded of the well-known Iranian novelist Moniro Ravanipour. I knew her in Iran, but we met at literary events where no one talked about personal matters. It was not until both of us migrated to the US that I got to know her better. When I first met her, she gave the impression of being in constant motion, making me feel as if within her thousands of darts were moving in different directions. Even when she was sitting down, I had the impression that she appeared in the periphery of my vision, then quickly disappeared, materializing in a different location.

In America, we communicated from time to time through phone and later email. It was then I realized that the state of restlessness and motion I had sensed in her was based on her life at the time, when she was literally on the run.

Her family had the bad luck of having political tendencies that did not suit the new revolutionary regime. She says in an interview how, in the first years of the revolution, her nineteen-year-old brother was executed ("shot through the heart"); her second sister and her husband were sentenced to death but managed to flee Iran; her older sister's husband was jailed four times; her twelve-year-old sister was arrested; and two other siblings, ages eleven and thirteen, were expelled from school.

There's more: her father's assets in the southern city of Bushehr were confiscated and their house looted. They moved to another city, Shiraz, and she herself was on the run. In a profile of Ravanipour, she says, "As a writer in Iran, I am a foreigner in my own country. They are looking for the enemy, and I am the enemy."

In her emails to me, Moniro talks about how she was constantly on the move from city to city, taking refuge in relatives' and friends' houses, spending more and more time in buses moving from one place to another. While staying at friends' and relatives' homes Moniro would ask her hosts to tell her their stories. "This was when I realized," she said, "that traveling, listening to other people's stories, and writing one's memories is a way of confronting depression and trauma. I very instinctively and automatically chose this in order to save my life." There was no hope of publishing what she wrote, but she pressed on because "I felt good, I felt alive. The thought of publishing was a distant mirage, incredible . . . like a miracle that finally happened to me."

She was on the run, until one day in spring of 1982, two weeks before the Iranian New Year on March 21, when she too was arrested. Luckily, her brother-in-law had gone to her place and destroyed all of her politically incriminating documents. She was not a published writer at the time. She says in an interview with Miranda Mellis that when she was in jail one night, she vowed that if she ever got out, she would write. "For years, I had completely forgotten about that night until I came to the US and realized that when I'm not writing anything, I feel short of breath. I returned to these memories and discovered that I write so they can't kill me; that I write to stay alive."

I share with Moniro this feeling that I survived through reading and writing, in a literal sense. Psychologically, at least, I can make that claim.

A TOTALITARIAN MINDSET, BE IT in a theocracy or a democracy, is the enemy of complication, of ambiguity. Maybe, Baba, this is one reason for my writing these letters to you, because of those contradictions and complexities, which in the kind of world we are living now are becoming more and more scarce— perhaps one kind of evil is a mind that allows no ambiguities, no complications. The totalitarian mindset convinces its victims that the world is black and white. And it is not. In her novels, Atwood gives us a subversive view of this black-

and-white world, where any form of opposition is met with elimination and death, and she reveals the complications, inconsistencies, and paradoxes that even the fanatics in the absolutist states cannot wholly evade: the Guardians who want a peek at the Handmaid's face; the Commander who uses his power and risks his position to play Scrabble with the Handmaid; the almost all-powerful Aunt who is secretly planning the destruction of Gilead. Suddenly, behind the seemingly immovable façade, there are all sorts of movements. Uncontrollable. Inevitable. This does not exonerate the enemy—the Commander is still a Commander, after all. But it does create hope, hope that one day the movements behind the façade will cause it to crack and then finally crumble. Recognition of this complexity—of the fact that your enemy, like you, is only human—is one of the most potent weapons against authoritarian mindsets. The more they dehumanize us, the more we should humanize them.

This is as true of democracies as it is of totalitarian systems. We see it when Donald Trump calls Democrats "scum" and Nancy Pelosi "Crazy Nancy," and Pelosi responds by saying she prays for him. She does not fall into his trap, she does not play the same game, and this puts her in a place of strength. In response to Hitler's concentration camps, the Allies created the Nuremberg trials. The trials were not perfect, but at least they showed an attitude opposite that of the Nazis: treating the enemy as human beings with legal rights. It was crucial that those who fought against Hitler and Fascists would not act like them after the victory over them. To have done so would have diminished the Allies, not their enemy.

In the black-and-white world of Gilead, Atwood introduces gradations of color. As readers, we hate this system that has created so much suffering, and we know that it must be destroyed. Yet when confronted with individuals within that same system, we discover that they are human like us, or that we are human like them. Not that they can be exonerated— not that the Commander shouldn't pay for his actions or that Aunt Lydia should be absolved—but that the best and surest way of fighting the system is refusing to see the world in black and white, instead offering our enemies what they have denied us: justice.

LATER IN THE EVENING, I take my cup of coffee out onto the balcony. It is cool, a caressing sort of cool. Alongside the river, I notice two bicycles, and a jogger, and, after a few minutes, a large, bright-yellow water taxi passing by. All calm and quiet on this front. I stand there watching, while in my mind a sentence keeps repeating itself. It is one I have often quoted in my talks, from Tzvetan Todorov's 1991 book *Facing the Extreme: Moral Life in the Concentration Camps:* "only total oblivion calls for total despair."

I was reminded of this line often as I reread *The Handmaid's Tale* and as I was reading what Atwood said in her *New York Times* piece about Offred's narrative. She tells us that Offred's account belongs to a literary form called witness literature. (David Grossman and James Baldwin also consider themselves witnesses.) "Offred records her story as best she can," Atwood writes, and "then she hides it, trusting that it may be discovered later by someone who is free to understand it and share it. This is an act of hope: every recorded story implies a future reader." Baba jan, I wonder if you wrote your diaries with this hope in mind.

Which goes to the heart of the relationship between readers and writers. Offred, talking to her unknown future reader, or, perhaps in her case, listener, tells her, "You don't tell a story only to yourself. There's always someone else. Even when there is no one." She goes even further and claims that she creates her reader: "By telling you anything at all I'm at least believing in you. I believe you're there, I believe you into being. Because I'm telling you this story, I will your existence. I tell, therefore you are."

Aunt Lydia expresses a similar idea as she ponders whether to continue collaborating or to betray Gilead. If she decides to collaborate then she will have to destroy her manuscript. "In that case," she tells her future reader, "I would destroy these pages I have written so laboriously; and I would destroy you along with them, my future reader." She adds almost gleefully, mischievously, "One flare of a match and you'll be gone— wiped away as if you had never been, as if you will never be. I would deny you existence. What a godlike feeling! Though it is a god of annihilation."

At the height of her despair, Offred, like so many people living through trauma, starts to record her life in Gilead, so as not to forget and not allow the future generations to forget. She's providing conclusive evidence that such things have happened, and she and many other victims have been witness to them, lived through them, lived in spite of them. We need to remember, despite the fact that every atom in our body wants to forget. Memory becomes one of the most potent weapons against the cruelty of totalitarian regimes and concentration camps. Todorov reminds us that telling and reading the story might not change the dire reality, but it makes us understand that reality, and it gives meaning to our lives, no matter how horrendous those lives have become. He writes, "Remember everything, and tell it, not just to fight against the camps but so that, having left something behind, our lives will have had some meaning."

"Only total oblivion calls for total despair." That is at the heart of the literature of witness. To me, the hope Atwood refers to is inherent in the act of storytelling. Readers become keepers of memory, keepers of truth.

So it is with hope that I end this letter, dear Baba, raising my cup of coffee to the witnesses and their stories.

With love
Baba's daughter,
Azi

BALDWIN, COATES

Dearest Baba,

I keep thinking of how you would have loved James Baldwin. Over the past two months, I have done little except for reading and rereading his work. I have piled his books, along with a few by other authors, in different corners of my bedroom. For some unknown reason I feel most comfortable reading them and writing about them there rather than in my office. With my other books, I often wrote in museums and coffee shops, sometimes in my office. I wonder if the pandemic has something to do with my retreat to my bedroom. Recently, I have extended my workplace to the balcony facing the river, when the weather is agreeable. A sort of psychological and emotional quarantine, withdrawing into safety, a cocoon that I hope will have the promise of flight.

I feel like writing a letter of introduction to both of you: James Baldwin, meet my father, Ahmad; Father, meet James. I think Baldwin would have appreciated your encounters with racism in America. I was always impressed by how, no matter which country you visited, you became immersed in the place, wanting to know everything about it. I remember when I was about eleven, you were going on a job-related trip to Germany for three months, and some months before your trip you started learning the language. Remember how you practiced it by talking to me in German?!

But I believe that no place mesmerized you as much as America did. I am thinking of all the discussions you and I have had about the United States, especially the problem of race in this country. You discuss it in your memoir. I was particularly taken by one event you mention there. You wrote that during your stay in America, studying at the American University, one day you were on your way to visit the US Office of Budget and Management, and it began raining. You took refuge under a huge, ancient tree near Blair House, the American presidents' guest house. There you met the doorman, a big African American guy with whom you started a conversation.

He was critical of the government and cynical about it doing anything for Black people. The man sounded angry about the ruling elite and said those in power were like gangsters, that they were mere fronts for the ones who robbed the people and monopolized the country's economy. You write in your memoirs that he told you, "I serve this institution, I am a hardworking staff member offering my services to the president. But I am not Ike's servant, I am free in expressing my views. If this president abolished racial prejudice, then I'll take my words back!"

Do you remember when we first discussed this encounter? You said that since the time you met that guard, you had seen enough racial prejudice to understand his rage. I was touched by the way you empathized with this man, how his sorrow became your sorrow. To me, his anguish got at the contradiction at the heart of America. On one hand, he considered himself free enough to so bitterly criticize his government to a stranger; on the other, he had good reason to feel that his country's policy makers were nothing more than gangsters. You once told me, "A country so dedicated to freedom, I just cannot understand how it can also be so cruel and unfree."

When you returned to Iran you must have continued to think about race in America, because I found out that while you were in jail, after having read President Lyndon Johnson's speech on the Great Society, you wrote him an open letter that was published in *Khandaniha*, the most politically independent publication in Iran. It would be translated into English by America's Office of Media and Public Relations. I remember that you had met Johnson when, as vice president, he visited Iran in 1963 while you were the mayor of Tehran. I don't want to quote you to yourself, but I was so moved by that letter, in which you linked racism in America to poverty and injustice, saying:

> I have seen the anxiety and agitation of striking workers in Detroit, watching them in deep distress, lying along streets with bottles of whiskey in their hands; I have observed the worn-out, sad, wistful residents of the ruined, grimy buildings covered with broken windows in Harlem and the Black neighborhoods of Chicago; I have empathized with America's castaway people of color on the Nineteenth Street of Washington; I have witnessed the sorrowful faces of the hungry, jobless workers on the docksides of New York, Baltimore, and New Orleans. Yet, I have also passed by the newly constructed buildings whose doors

open automatically in front of people and whose façade, as well
as internal facilities, signify their owners' utmost comfort and
well-being; I have enjoyed the infinite blessings of individual
freedom in your land and relished the beautiful parks, luxurious
theaters, magnificent restaurants, excellent cars and airplanes,
as well as the comfortable life in your country—and having
witnessed all those, I am very much eager to see the person
whose thoughts I briefly recounted here win the election.

Around the same time you were studying in the States,
Baldwin was writing about race and racism in America and
how African Americans' destiny was also America's destiny.
So you see why I am convinced that you and Baldwin would
have gotten along famously.

Thirty years after James Baldwin's death, in an era that
has brought to the surface all sorts of hidden, festering, and
hate-filled sentiments, his work has never felt more relevant—
and disturbing. He once said that the writer, the artist, is
a disturber of the peace, and I believe that if we are not
disturbed by him today, we have missed the point. His point.

When I was writing about Baldwin in *The Republic of
Imagination* (2014), I read a piece in the *New York Times* about
the waning interest in Baldwin among African American
youth. But now there are many out there who, like me, feel
that these times are Baldwin's times. Books have been written
about him or been inspired by him. His 1974 novel *If Beale
Street Could Talk* was turned into a celebrated film in 2018,
following the release of a new documentary about his life and
work, among other celebrations of his art and activism. There
are many positive aspects to all this. At the same time, I fear

that there is a danger in so much attention that is partly aimed at making him more comfortable to "be around." I am not sure that those of us paying homage to Baldwin are fully aware of the fact that his work, in its critique of America, is not just a critique of the obvious villains in the story. Rather, it is a criticism of an attitude, a mindset that any one of us could have and which dominates America today.

SINCE I WROTE YOU LAST, so many things have happened. Suddenly the ominous and insidious silence of the pandemic has been broken by a different kind of tragedy: a young Black man named George Floyd was murdered by the Minneapolis police. We watched a video, showing Floyd lying on the ground while one officer presses his knee into the handcuffed man's neck, and three other officers stand there watching. Mr. Chauvin kept his knee on George Floyd's neck for nine minutes and twenty nine seconds while Floyd kept saying "I can't breathe."

Immediately, protests erupted throughout the country. Floyd was only the latest known casualty in a long line of other Black victims of police violence, and protests had been voiced in those cases, but never to this extent and never for this duration. Tens of thousands poured into the streets of different cities, protesting police brutality and violence against African Americans. The situation was exacerbated by Trump threatening to use force and the National Guard against the protestors, warning of "vicious dogs" and "ominous weapons."

Over the past several days, the protests have been going on full force. I can't sleep or eat; I mainly pace around our apartment, hopeful but anxious. Just try to imagine it, Baba jan, tens of thousands, mainly youth, from all different races and ethnicities, are marching through the streets of this country, demanding justice.

Before this last tragedy, there was a series of incidents where Blacks were killed by the police: Tamir Rice, Michael Brown, Philando Castile, Eric Garner, Trayvon Martin, Breonna Taylor, and too many others to mention. All these killings were followed by outrage and protest, but after a while, things went back to "normal," until the next killing. This time feels different: the protests keep gaining momentum, and they go beyond police brutality. The very texture of these protests is different from before, as if they had soaked up all the outrage of previous protests. One noteworthy fact is that more than ever the protestors come from different races, genders, and age groups. This is the point where the majority of Americans will converge. No wonder James Baldwin is back among us, alive and well, more needed than ever.

Baldwin is being quoted on those streets. Reading him and writing about him during this time gives me an opportunity to understand more clearly the rage behind the protests. He had said, "To be a Negro in this country and to be relatively conscious is to be in a rage almost all the time." But the point is that while he so well captures the rage, he also gives direction to it and channels it into something positive, into real change.

Baba jan, I keep talking to you mainly of our lives of fear and anxiety in the Islamic Republic, but there was a moment when I found myself as frightened here in the

United States as I had been in the Islamic Republic of Iran. The fear and anxiety I feel now is a continuation of how I felt in 2017 as I watched the events unfold in Charlottesville, Virginia, surrounding the demonstrations and march of white nationalists. The images from that rally frightened me, all those angry white men, carrying torches, Nazi flags, rifles, and hurling racist slogans were terrifying. Those demonstrations had ended in violence as James Alex Fields Jr., a white supremist sympathizer, crashed his car into the counterprotesters, killing Heather D. Heyer and injuring thirty others.

There was the shock: Where had these people been hiding? How could we not have known that they were out there? Were these our next-door neighbors? Had we underestimated how dangerous Trump really is? I realized, in that moment, that this was indeed a fight for the soul of America. We mostly expect from politicians the offer of changes in policy, when what we need is a fundamental change in attitude—after all, any change in policy is based on a specific attitude and mindset. We need the words of a visionary. We need someone to unite us beyond politics. Baldwin had once written, "It is certain in any case that ignorance, allied with power, is the most ferocious enemy justice can have." And here I was experiencing, as I did in Iran, the effects of "ignorance allied with power."

African Americans have lived with similar fears and the anger that accompanies it—now, once more, the anger has come to the surface, but now, more than ever before, they share it with Americans of different races, genders, ages, and backgrounds. Yesterday I talked to Negar about the evil of "ignorance allied with power," the evil of power. She said, "Don't forget the power of evil." We did underestimate it. I said, it always counts on that: on us underestimating it.

I FIRST READ BALDWIN IN another time of deep unrest and protests. It was during college at the University of Oklahoma in the 1970s. As I mentioned in a previous letter, I was active in many protests, from the war in Vietnam, to anti-shah activities. And you too must remember those times, because in Iran, you were warned and interrogated a few times by the secret police about my political activities abroad.

How ironic that you, who stood up to the government for more than four years, refusing to compromise in exchange for your freedom, would be so worried and anxious about my political involvement, trying to warn me of the danger of my activities on the OU campus. If I remember correctly, you felt the young people's rebellion in America against the government was as much about lifestyle as it was about politics. It seemed to me at the time that you were puzzled by the young protestors, who seemed to embrace such disparate causes, from opposition to the Vietnam war and the CIA, to support for smoking pot, even going streaking on college campuses.

Do you remember while you visited me in Norman in the early seventies you and I went to see the film *The Sting,* starring Paul Newman and Robert Redford? I will never forget that in the middle of the film suddenly someone started running naked down the aisle shouting slogans! I now better understand what you meant when you told me that as far as our protests against war, racism, sexism, and corporate greed

went, you were with me. But, you said, you can't talk about
the negative aspects of society without mentioning the positive
sides, the parts that bring to your attention the possibilities
and the hope for change.

I wish I had taken your words more seriously when you
talked about these possibilities you felt existed in the idea of
democracy in America and its promise. You told me that those
like Dr. Martin Luther King Jr. have used the promise and
freedoms of America to fight against the brutality and violence
of racism, and disenfranchised people in the future should do
the same.

In those days I did not pay much attention to what you
said about the possibilities and promises of America. The
American branch of the Confederation of Iranian Students,
the organization I was active in, was too rigid and puritanical
to leave much room for complexities and ambiguities. Nor
could I reconcile my activities in the confederation with my
passion for literature and the arts. Within the organization, I
was responsible mainly for cultural activities and international
relations, which involved collaborating with other radical
groups and organizations both American and international.
I kept myself busy shouting slogans against the war while
watching movies by Fellini and Bergman and plays by
Edward Albee and Jean Genet; listening to the Doors, Jimi
Hendrix, Janis Joplin, and the Mothers of Invention; writing
tracts against the shah; listening to Black activists Stokely
Carmichael and H. Rap Brown; and reading *Madame Bovary*,
To the Lighthouse, *Tom Jones*, and Eldridge Cleaver's *Soul on
Ice*. I have always found it ironic that Cleaver, initially an early
leader of the Black Panther Party, a radical, and a fugitive, who
called Baldwin a "faggot," a "reluctant black," and "a white man

in a black body," turned out in the end to be a Republican and a member of the Church of Jesus Christ of Latter-day Saints.

Baldwin's words back then connected me to these protest movements, while at the same time taking me out of them and into a different space, where I could slow down, internalize, and reflect. Where my thoughts and actions were not simply ruled by rage. Without realizing it fully at the time, I admired Baldwin because of the way he mercilessly criticized the blatant racism in America yet did not give himself wholly to a political group or ideology. Rather, he preserved his independence of mind. Baldwin proved to me that being a dedicated writer didn't have to mean compromising one's political independence—writers question all established norms, including the political ones. I don't mean that we should not get involved in politics, but the best way is to refuse to blindly follow the party line.

You, of course, would understand what I am saying, having paid the price by spending four years of your life in jail because you did not give up your political independence. A writer such as Baldwin is different from some ideological revolutionaries, because more than having prefabricated answers, he poses unanswered questions. He believed "all theories are suspect, that the finest principles may have to be modified, or may even be pulverized by the demands of life, and that one must find, therefore, one's own moral center and move through the world hoping that this center will guide one aright."

Squirrel-like, after college, I stored Baldwin's words in the back of my mind and did not return to them for two decades. Then in 1997, after immigrating to the United States, I started rereading his work, while at the same time immersing myself in American history. For a while, I read him obsessively, almost maniacally—his books, his interviews, his reviews.

The more anxious I became about the state of affairs in America, the more I read Baldwin and filled notebooks writing about him, jotting down quotes from him. This obsession was partly appeased while writing my book *The Republic of Imagination*. I ended that book with an epilogue on Baldwin. I felt it was fitting that a book which begins with Mark Twain should end with James Baldwin. There were many reasons why I wrote the epilogue about him, one being that I felt he was not just a great African American or gay writer, but a great writer. I believe his first novel, 1953's *Go Tell It on the Mountain*, deserves the title of the Great American Novel. Like *The Adventures of Huckleberry Finn* and more than J. D. Salinger's *Catcher in the Rye*, Baldwin had created not only a new American protagonist in the person of John Grimes but also a new language.

After *The Republic of Imagination* was published, however, I still felt I had some unfinished business with him—that it was not the end of our conversation. Baldwin's words really did hit me like a gut punch. I believe that having lived in the Islamic Republic had something to do with the way I reacted to his work, to his words. I had found an affinity. He talked once about how he connected to the rage in Dickens's work, and *Uncle Tom's Cabin*, saying there was something in them that "I recognized without knowing what I recognized." That's how I felt about Baldwin's own work.

Dear Baba, let me explain what I mean. Do you remember how, back in the Islamic Republic, violence and rage were part and parcel of our daily lives, so much so that we no longer registered them as exceptional? The shock of living under such conditions had made us almost numb and paralyzed. The story I am going to tell is nothing exceptional for you and I who lived there—so unexceptional that I never mentioned it to you. It is only in hindsight that it sounds so horrible, so intolerable. In fact, I like to call it "An Evening Like Any Other in the Islamic Republic of Iran."

It was past midnight, and Bijan and I were driving home from a friend's house. (You know them: Shayda and Mansour Miri.) Earlier that evening, they had invited us for a swim and then dinner. As usual, over dinner we shared stories, followed by speculation and debates. Shayda and her husband told us that two weeks earlier they had been arrested at a party, taken to see the Revolutionary Committee in a bus, and kept at the Revolutionary Committee's headquarters for three nights, before they paid a huge amount of money for their release. Their crime: participating in a mixed-gender party with booze and music. We all raised our glasses and celebrated the fact that our hosts had gotten off so easy—after all, they weren't flogged or jailed—counting our blessings, knowing that it could have been much worse.

At some point over dessert and coffee—the Islamic regime was never able to destroy Iran's pastry and ice cream—I felt anger rising in me. The fact that we considered our hosts lucky, that having to bribe officials to avoid punishment was now an accepted norm, and that such incidents were a part of everyday life, infuriated me. We knew that others were in jail for defending human rights, for writing the truth, and that some were being tortured, some were being executed, and, in cases involving adultery or prostitution, stoned to death. And there we were, swimming and enjoying pastry.

Something was wrong, apart from the obvious fact that

everything in that cursed land was wrong at that moment. There was something that went deeper; something that, like my anger, had no specific shape or form. I would realize later what it was: complicity. Yes, the regime was the main instigator of the tragedy we lived in, responsible for the misery, fear, and desperation that had become part of our daily lives. The question was: How could we live under the rule of this regime, without being contaminated by its corruption? Could we survive without kowtowing to a system that tried to control every aspect of our lives? Could we remain morally intact in a place where immorality was not just the norm but the rule? One of the things that made the Islamic regime so intolerable was what it did to its citizens morally and spiritually, draining us of our sense of right or wrong, making us complicit even in the crimes committed against us. And today, more than two decades later, I find it sadly ironic that I ask the same questions and suffer from the same misgivings here and now in the United States of America, where, during these protests, so many Americans are asking the same questions we asked about life in the Islamic Republic of Iran.

On the drive home, Bijan and I were quiet. I felt a bit exhausted and vaguely unhappy. Then we saw the roadblock. It was nothing unusual; in those days, roadblocks and searches, not just for weapons but also for political tracts, music, and alcohol, were part of life. We knew enough to take precautions and never to carry cassettes or alcoholic beverages in the car, or to raise our voices when interrogated. Despite the routine nature of such searches, they still made me angry. But also fearful: I automatically checked my scarf, making sure it covered my hair in the proper manner.

A bearded elderly man holding a gun, and two young boys,

also with guns, signaled us to stop. We did. Bijan rolled down the window and was then ordered to get out of the car. After some minutes, they told me to also get out. Without even looking at him properly, I knew that the older man would be wearing sandals and have his shirt untucked over his trousers. The fact that they didn't wear a uniform but all uniformly appeared this way made it all more eerie. I knew that he was addressed not by an official title but by the term applied to those who had been on the holy pilgrimage to Mecca, Haj Agha, by the young ones who were standing behind him, stiffly holding their rifles. I couldn't take my eyes off their guns, which seemed to have become extensions of their bodies like fingers on a hand. I was disturbed by how young the boys with him were, mere teenagers.

Haj Agha asked us the usual questions about where we had been, whether we'd been drinking, and if we had any cassettes. We gave him the usual answers, then they searched the car and the trunk. Finally, one of them pointed his gun our way and signaled that we could go. Once more we had been lucky!

All of this I now write in the calm of my home in DC, with a cup of coffee by my side and Bessie Smith on my stereo singing the "Reckless Blues" (in Baldwin's honor, obviously). On the evening when Bijan and I were stopped, I was quite out of touch with how the encounter made me feel. There is a numbness in moments of trauma that helps you get through the traumatic event. Paradoxically, sometimes my feelings were so intense, so overwhelming, that I felt numb.

If one of these young boys that we met on our nightly excursions around the city had held his gun to my head and fired, there likely would have been no consequences for him.

Our utter helplessness, the fact that we were not only forced to hide our outrage and suppress any sort of reaction to what was happening, but that we also had to be polite—and not merely polite but ingratiating—was what was so intolerable. At almost every one of these checkpoint encounters, unlike the feeling of numbness I felt on the surface, the deeper emotions I was experiencing were the same: a feeling of hatred, of outrage so overwhelming that I wished that gun in Haj Agha's hand was mine.

I ask myself: Is it because of my experiences in the Islamic Republic that I feel such kinship with James Baldwin? The mechanisms of oppression are basically the same, although they very much differ in degree and form: the victim is defined as different and alien, and therefore dangerous. That might have intensified my feelings about Baldwin, but surely it cannot be the only explanation for the way I react to his fiction and essays.

At some point, a particular experience gains a universal context. On one level, I feel that Baldwin's writing has illuminated my inarticulate anger, reassuring me that my experiences in the Islamic Republic have a universal context. But my preoccupation with him was based not only on a sense of identity, but also it grew out of his ability to draw me out of myself and to make me want to know and understand his experiences, which were so different from my own. Isn't this what great literature does: drawing upon our shared humanity while also pointing to our differences? His essays offered me a new perspective on race and racism, and on America as well, and I became more curious about what he meant when he said he was not a spokesperson but a witness to truth.

For me, dear Baba, Baldwin's vision about the relation between race and freedom in America was intriguing. He believed that for race relations in America to change, America itself had to fundamentally change. The universal appeal of his words plus the excitement of discovery, of something new, even if painful and complicated, drew me to his work. And the way he used the language felt like magic. I connected to him through both my heart and my head.

MY EXPERIENCE AT THE CHECKPOINT has something in common with Baldwin's experiences of racism, which made him boiling over with hatred and fear; hatred of the blatant act of racism, and fear of not just the very real menace of white folks out to get him but also fear of his own hatred, of what it might make him do—"afraid of the evil within me and afraid of the evil without," as he had written in his essay "Letter from a Region in My Mind." He had claimed in *The Fire Next Time*, "Hatred which could destroy so much, never failed to destroy the man who hated, and this was an immutable law." Is it any wonder that some return to Baldwin and quote him at a time like this when the streets are filled with protesters demanding justice? It sometimes appears that in such cases the victim must choose between remaining a victim or giving in to hatred. Baldwin seems to reject both. He resists giving in to the impulse he describes in his critique of Richard Wright's *Native Son*, in a piece titled "Nothing Personal," published in his 1985 book of essays *Price of the Ticket*, where Baldwin says of the novel's protagonist, Bigger, that he "is controlled, defined by his hatred and his fear," and "his fear drives him to murder and his hatred to rape." I wonder if it was fear and hatred, or was it fear of what he might be driven to do that motivated Baldwin to leave New York for Paris?

Each time I read or reread Baldwin expressing his rage and hatred, I experience the same odd mixture of relief and exasperation. I'm reminded of scenes from my own past, like that night at the checkpoint, or my reaction to the Islamic regime's quashing of protests, and I recognize how right he was to fear himself. I know how very hard it is to keep hatred in check, to resist succumbing to it. "It has always been much easier (because it has always seemed much safer)," he wrote, in "Nothing Personal," "to give a name to the evil without than to locate the terror within. And yet, the terror within is far truer and far more powerful than any of our labels: the labels change, the terror is constant."

I remember a phone conversation I had with Shirin, my friend in Iran. I tried to tell her about how angry I had been and how worried I was that anger would be the only feeling I would have; that I would be unable to turn my hatred into something constructive. She said that I was overintellectualizing and that I should say what I'd just told her to the families of the 1,500 people killed by the regime in the November 2019 protests. "People are angry," she said. "That is all they have. Let us not try to take that away from them."

She noted that people in Iran are so angry that many support Donald Trump because of his anti-Iran policies, preferring him to Biden. I said, "Well, the same is true of some Iranians here, but I don't agree with them. To begin with, I don't trust anyone who talks about human rights in other places but does not practice them in his or her own country. Look at the way Trump treated the immigrants or the people coming to America from Muslim-majority countries."

Shirin said, "I get that, but I also get Iranian people's anger. I find it quite legitimate." Then suddenly her somber tone changed and became much livelier. "By the way," she asked, "have you read a book called *Compass* by this French author called Enard? It is quite interesting and different."

This is Shirin for you: no matter how terrible she feels, a good book always perks her up. Baba jan, I rely on her to keep me updated. Since I returned to America, I have little information about books published in languages other than English. In Iran, we were much more cosmopolitan, reading works from all over the world. Rather sad that the world knows so much about America, while America knows so little about the world.

After my conversation with Shirin, I had a good talk with Negar, who told me that racism is like a disease: you need to be cleansed of it in order to be cured. The rage helps with the cleansing, the rage needs an outlet, and the protests are the outlet. We will go beyond them, and, through them, we will find our way, we will organize and reorganize.

Some might say that reading—even reading someone like Baldwin—will not help us in these times, which are times for action and not reading. I would say that such reading is part of the action. It is important to know how to direct the rage, rather than allowing the rage to direct you, and how to sustain the struggle, and overcome the obstacles it presents. I agree with Shirin: we cannot do away with anger. But I also agree with Negar that we can channel our rage into something constructive, the way that you, Baba, did in jail, where you took up painting, learned new languages, read, and wrote. Or the way that Baldwin, through writing, gave shape to his rage and gained some measure of control over it.

BABA JAN, I CAN'T SLEEP at night. No matter what I do and what I am thinking, the pandemic and the violence that killed George Floyd are lurking in a corner of my mind. The protests, oddly enough, calm me down. They give me hope, hope not as simple optimism but as Vaclav Havel's definition of it: "Hope is not the conviction that something will turn out well but the certainty that something makes sense, regardless of how it turns out."

This kind of hope comes to mind when I think of a Black man named Patrick Hutchinson, who seems like a protagonist out of a Baldwin novel. During Black Lives Matter protests in London, Hutchinson and his friends noticed an injured white man, whom Hutchison said he knew was not there to support Black Lives matter and was, in fact, "up to no good, let's just say." The man was being hit by some protestors. Hutchinson picked him up and, with friends, formed a wall of bodies around him, protecting him so that they could carry him to a police station. Hutchinson later said, "My real focus was on avoiding a catastrophe, all of a sudden the narrative changes into 'Black Lives Matters, Youngsters Kill Protestors.' That was the message we were trying to avoid." He also said that his main goal was "equality for everybody. . . . The world I live in has been better than my grandparents' and my parents', and, hopefully, we can continue until we have total equality for everyone." For him, "Just because somebody's up to no good, doesn't mean you have to kill them." It is this Baldwinian generosity of spirit that makes me hopeful about the future of the protests.

But still I worry. Iran has taught me, and America is teaching me again through the pandemic and its current crisis, about the fragility of life and how easy it is to lose everything that makes you safe and secure, how easy it is for the walls in the place you call home to crumble over your head. I first discovered this when you went to jail, Baba jan: that there were forces beyond my control that could take away from me all my protections. My only hope is that no matter how out of control things become, we have the will in one respect: in the attitude we choose to confront the fragility of life and the absoluteness of death. Which is one reason I read and write about James Baldwin.

IT IS SUMMER 2020. The virus has subsided a little, and we can meet in open air, though we still observe social distancing. Negar called a few minutes ago to invite us to their place next Sunday—we will be outside, each of us seating six feet apart from others! She then asked, "Mom, what are you doing?" I explained that I was writing you, her grandfather, a letter. I told her I was telling you about Baldwin and how Baldwin involves me through his writing. The passion of his words, I told her, is contagious. She said, on the subject of passion, that one thing she really appreciated about you was how you made us participate in things you were passionate about. She said you also involved her and Dara in the stories you told.

"He never just told us a story," she said, "He made us participate in it. In the middle of storytelling, he would pause with a question, asking you, for example, what you would have done were you such-and-such a character in the story he was telling." She is right. That was why we had so much fun with you. And you did this not just with stories but also with gardening, for example, one of your great passions. You would explain to us what you were doing, and before you know it, we had joined you in planting the herbs or flowers. All through our childhood, you created memories for us, something I wanted to do with my children. My God, how I wish you could see Negar's garden. I believe with you that gardens are living entities and have souls. Her garden glows and blooms and has the self-confidence of a well-loved and well taken care of child.

BABA JAN, WHEN I AM not writing, I am glued to the news. One moment, I am taken by the extent and diversity of the demonstrations, of the eloquent presentation of their demand: to not be defined and judged by the color of their skin. The next moment, I am enraged by the National Guard deploying tear gas on the peaceful demonstrators, dispersing them so that Trump and his entourage could walk from the White House to the church nearby for a photo op with Trump holding a Bible outside the church. I also know that so much depends on the direction of these protests, of their refusal to give in to rage and hatred, of their following the path of James Baldwin and Martin Luther King. Writing you allows me some distance from the outside reality so that I can digest it. What is happening out there is so intense that the events transcend metaphor; they put a full stop to words.

A few days ago, I was talking to an Iranian friend who lives in the US, and she said we should not get too involved in the protests here, as we have our own protests and situation back in Iran to think about. I don't agree with her. First of all, I am now an American citizen, an Iranian American, and have a stake in what happens here, plus the fact that I feel the protests in the two countries I have called home are related and nourish each other, although perhaps they don't seem to be. The search for justice and freedom in any part of the world enriches and encourages the search for justice and freedom the world over. In the same manner, those on the side of oppression are strengthened by oppression in other parts of the world.

As a woman, teacher, writer, and reader, having lived in the Islamic Republic, I have experienced segregation, discrimination, censorship, and oppression. But above all, as a human being, a believer in human rights and freedoms, an immigrant who has experienced the lack of rights and freedoms in her own country *and* supported the fight for them, I will actively support the fight for democracy no matter in which part of the world it is fought, especially in a country I now call mine. Well, now I feel much better after this harangue! More effective than coffee and brandy!

It is interesting that Shirin, who still lives in Iran, feels more invested in America's fate than my friend who lives here. Shirin not only knows about the latest books and films coming out of America, but also she follows its political and social issues meticulously. She was telling me the other day that Trump, like the virus, is contagious: deadly not only for America but also for the rest of the world.

WHEN I READ *BETWEEN THE WORLD AND ME*, by the African American writer and journalist Ta-Nehisi Coates, I again thought of James Baldwin. Coates's book, addressed to his fifteen-year-old son, Samori, was inspired by Baldwin's "A Letter to My Nephew," published in *Progressive* magazine in 1962. Coates is someone who has followed Baldwin's dangerous path to truth but is not an imitator; instead, he is his own man. Like Baldwin, he is aware of the dangers lurking within: "Perhaps I too had the capacity for plunder, maybe I would take another human's body to confirm myself in a community. Perhaps I already had."

Like Baldwin, Coates believes it is his duty to hold his country accountable for its deep-seated racism—precisely because it is his country. Coates confronts those who would justify America's history with the claim that all nations have at one time or another committed acts of oppression and plunder. He rejects this excuse, and eloquently condemns America's actions by citing its own claims:

> Perhaps there has been, some point in history, some great power whose elevation was exempt from the violent exploitation of other human bodies. If there has been, I have yet to discover it. But this banality of violence can never excuse America, because America makes no claim to the banal. America believes itself exceptional, the greatest and noblest nation ever to exist, a lone champion standing between the white city of democracy and the terrorists, despots, barbarians, and other enemies of civilization. One cannot, at once, claim to be superhuman and then plead mortal error.

For both writers, it begins with race. Like Baldwin, Coates believes there is no inherent biological basis to race, and that white and Black are political constructs, a ploy created to ensure the subjugation of one group of people by another.

"But race is the child of racism, not the father," he says. Baldwin claims that as long as the people insist that they are white, he has no choice but to remain Black. Even in his late writing, where he has become far more disenchanted with the struggle, he still keeps faith in his basic belief that race is a construct and that the solution to racism comes through both Black and white people. In his introduction to *The Price of the Ticket*, Baldwin says, "White people are not white: part of the price of the white ticket is to delude themselves into believing that they are." And yet, as he says, racism has long defined all Americans. To begin with, dear Baba, racism negates the claims of the first few lines of the Declaration of Independence, that all men are created equal.

The way I see it, Baba jan, racism is a way to redefine a people, to keep them frozen within that false definition, turning them into an image dreamed up by another that has nothing to do with them, who they are, what they aspire to. It may not be just physical violence, but it is still a violence that corrupts the soul. The writing of both Baldwin and Coates fights against that attitude, that worldview, that mindset where the victim becomes infected with the hatred and rage generated by the oppressor—the kind that made me wish that Haj Agha's gun was mine that night at the checkpoint.

COATES GIVES A BRILLIANT DIAGNOSIS of the disease. I empathize with him in his rage and despair, wondering where the cycle of violence will end. He tells his son to struggle, but he does not explain in concrete terms how to defy and resist. He believes that the struggle should go on without investing in or inviting the participation of white people (those he calls "Dreamers"). Addressing his son, he says of the white people, "I do not believe we can stop them, Samori, because they must ultimately stop themselves," adding, "And still I urge you to struggle." Five years after *Between the World and Me* was published in 2015, it seems that the Dreamers have learnt a few lessons, and this has brought Coates new hope.

In an interview with Ezra Klein on Vox in June 2020, Coates makes the case that in the Floyd protests, in contrast to the civil rights protests of 1968, "I feel like more people get it, I feel like more people understand it." He also said: "I think a critical mass of nonblack people have come to see the enforcers of the state in a different kind of way." And: "George Floyd is not new. The ability to broadcast it the way it was broadcasted is new."

There is a thread that connects Coates to Baldwin despite the differences, including age and the times each lived in. Baldwin experienced the 1960s and the civil rights movement and the despair that came with it. If the survival of America is, as Baldwin has claimed, dependent on the "Negro struggle," then that struggle will be dependent on the participation of all Americans regardless of race. After all, from the very beginning of the fight against slavery until today, white people like Abraham Lincoln, Benjamin Lay, and John Brown and most of the prominent white women suffragettes, such as Elizabeth Cady Stanton, Ernestine Rose, Susan B. Anthony, and Lucretia Mott, have been in their own way part of that fight.

And Baldwin believed in a struggle in which both white and Black people participate. In a 1964 interview mainly

on the Black revolution and racism in America, with Robert
Penn Warren, Baldwin said, "You can despise white people.
You may even have given moments when you want to kill
them. But here it's your brothers and sisters, whether or not
they know that they are your brothers and sisters. And that
complicates it." He adds, "It complicates it so much that I
can't quite see my way through this." In *The Fire Next Time*, he
writes, "If we—and now I mean the relatively conscious whites
and the relatively conscious blacks, who must, like lovers,
insist or create, the consciousness of others—do not falter in
our duty now, we may be able, handful that we are, to end
the racial nightmare, and achieve our country and change the
history of the world." These words he uttered so many decades
ago remain relevant to us today.

Coates also at one point has experienced the despair, but
the hope that the Black Lives Matter movement has ignited
in him has given him a new perspective in the fight against
racism. In his interview with Klein, he claims: "Even when I
was writing *Between the World and Me*, and certainly more so
since then, I have come to believe in the deep, moral case most
effectively made by King for nonviolence: that you actually
don't want to repeat what the people who are oppressing you
are doing. That when you do violence to someone else, there
is something corrupting about it. That's a very true thing. But
often it is the very people who squelch nonviolent protest who
then turn around and preach nonviolence."

The point that we should not act like our oppressors is a
given, but how to change the violence inflicted on us by the
oppressors, by those who claim we should remain nonviolent,
that is the question. The people asked to be nonviolent are
those with the ability to do the "least amount of damage,"

while we don't call upon people "who have the most power
and actually can do the most damage." This is a question,
Baba jan, I have been grappling with in relation to the Islamic
Republic. I don't want to become like them, to use violence,
but it gets complicated, especially when they shoot into
peaceful demonstrations, when any form of nonviolent protest
is met with violence. It is all easier said than done.

I AM STRUCK BY HOW clearly Baldwin saw things, even when
he was in deep despair about the success of the fight for civil
rights. Despite his disillusionment with changing attitudes
against racism in America in the last years of his life, Baldwin
did not exclude those of certain nationalities, ethnicities, or
backgrounds from writing or talking about race. He judged
people based on their values and principles in deeds as well as
in words.

For instance, he was the one, who, amidst criticism
of William Styron's 1967 novel about Nat Turner's slave
uprising, *The Confessions of Nat Turner*, defended Styron's
right to write about a heroic slave. Interviewed for the *Paris
Review* in 1984, he said that Styron writes for reasons similar
to his: "something which hurt him and frightened him." He
felt that Styron, like him, was trying to confront his history.
He even moderated a discussion between Styron and the
actor Ossie Davis in which Baldwin defended Styron's right
"to a confrontation with his history," saying, "No one has a
right to tell a writer what to write." In a remembrance that
Styron wrote for the *New York Times* following Baldwin's
passing, he recounted that they both believed "the writer
should be free to demolish the barrier of color, to cross the

forbidden line and write from the point of view of someone with a different skin."

I REALLY ADMIRE BALDWIN'S GIFT for going deep into the particulars of the African American experience, while at the same time drawing a universal response from readers. He never claimed that *Go Tell It on the Mountain* was specific only to the Black experience. For him, it was a gateway to writing fiction. He wanted to be a *writer*, not only a Black writer or a gay writer. For the act of writing in itself is also a call for universality, an appeal to those other than ourselves to engage in an experience, to share a story. In the kind of world we live in today, this is dangerous writing, which makes Baldwin's books dangerous reading. I call Baldwin's writing dangerous because instead of writing as a confirmation of what he knows, he writes to discover and confront what he does not know. He said, "When you're writing, you're trying to find out something which you don't know. The whole language of writing for me is finding out what you don't want to know, what you don't want to find out. But something forces you anyway." Instead of staying in his comfort zone and writing only from the Black perspective, 1956 saw Baldwin publish *Giovanni's Room*, about a white gay man living in Paris. In a 1980 interview, he characterized the novel as "not so much about homosexuality; it is what happens if you are so afraid that you finally cannot love anybody." In a letter to a friend, he mentions that *Giovanni's Room* was a book about America and American "loneliness and insecurity" rather than homosexuality.

Dear Baba, I want to tell you about Baldwin's novel

Another Country, from 1962. As I see it, in that book he attempts to shape his vision of a few "good whites" and a "few good blacks" getting together. The characters—a group of close friends both white and Black—and the challenges they face remind us in many ways of our challenges and problems today. It is an important novel, a poignantly beautiful one, and, I believe, his most ambitious. I wish you had read it, Baba jan; it would have led to one of those discussions I always looked forward to. He brings so many levels and complications to the story, avoiding the simplistic approach of the "protest novel"—the kind of novel that is based on a political agenda and ideology and usually has a political message. Here is my take on *Another Country*: racism is destructive, destroying the soul of both the perpetrator and the victim. The central character around whom this theme unfolds is Rufus Scott, a talented, young Black jazz drummer. Rufus, according to Baldwin, "is the black corpse floating in the national psyche." He represents the kind of despair many young Black men feel today, when a tragedy like George Floyd's murder reminds them of how unsafe life is for them in the place they call home.

Rufus falls for a poor white southern woman named Leona, whom he both loves and hates. Because she loves him, he despises her. In Rufus, we see how an intelligent and sensitive soul is gradually destroyed by the racism that envelops him. He hates the system that does this to him, but he simultaneously hates himself—and hates those who love him. Deep down, he knows that the inferiority attributed to him is not true, but he is still beholden to that image. He reaches a point when he cannot tolerate his way of life and kills himself by jumping off a bridge. Baldwin once said that he wanted

to show Rufus as partly responsible for his own downfall
and death. Because if he had no responsibility in shaping
his own fate, then there would be no hope for any of the
other characters who survive him. Amazing how, despite his
justified rage against racism, Baldwin could see the complexity
inherent in people and issues—to be so clear eyed must have
been both a blessing and a burden.

Baba jan, the main theme of the book is not unfamiliar
to the two of us. In *Another Country*, Baldwin returns to
his favorite and central theme: how a victim can come to
hate himself and see himself through his oppressor's eyes—
how hatred becomes infectious, like a virus. Not one of
the characters, whether Black or white, is comfortable in
her or his skin. I wonder how you would have reacted to
Another Country, considering that it explores some of the
most explosive themes of its times: bisexuality, interracial
couples, extramarital affairs. Each character, despite his or
her attempts at denials, has to face up to the truth, no matter
how painful. Rufus, who could not tolerate the truth of his
Blackness, commits suicide, and the rest have to deal with the
fallout. Cass must own up to the fact that her beloved novelist
husband, Richard, is not as dedicated to his writing as she
believed, and that his book, although popular, is a sham. Ada,
Rufus's beautiful sister, sleeps with Ellis, a powerful white
man in the entertainment industry, in order to get ahead in
the music world, despite being in love with another white
man, Vivaldo. The moment of truth for Vivaldo, also a writer,
and Rufus's best friend, comes when Ada tells him about
Ellis. Eric is the calmest and most centered of them all; he is
bisexual, has a steady relationship with another man, but, by
the end of the novel is unsure if that relation will last. *Another*

Country does not offer any easy solutions. In fact, in the end, all the relationships remain in limbo.

IT'S NOT AS IF ALL the violence and hate related to race in America did not have its adverse effects on Baldwin. At times, he appeared to lose hope, to believe that nothing would ever change. Following the assassinations of Martin Luther King Jr., Medgar Evers, and Malcolm X, and, after witnessing the brutal treatment of so many innocent African Americans during the struggles of the civil rights movement, it seems Baldwin reached a depth of despair similar to Coates's in *Between the World and Me* over the common struggle carried by both Blacks and whites. Baldwin said, after King's assassination, that "something has altered in me, something has gone away." And in *A Rap on Race*, a beautiful give-and-take conversation with Margaret Mead in 1970 filled with the kind of tension that arises out of an exchange based on both the intellect and the heart, he said that his hope for change in this country ended with MLK's death. At one point in their conversation, he suggested that he would change America by blowing it up.

Margaret Mead challenged him on this in that interview, and I want to challenge him on that specific outburst, especially now in this time of constant vacillation between despair and hope, when so much is at stake for the future of not just America but also the world. Because if the only way Baldwin can change this country is by blowing it up, the only way I can change anything would be by having that gun in my hand, and I know that won't change a damn thing. Baba, you and I have experienced the truth of this, having lived through a revolution and a war.

Dear Baba, we are once again living in an age of uncertainty. I believe the present state of affairs in this country is not because the civil rights movement failed but because of all that has been gained in its aftermath—as demonstrated by the successful Black Lives Matter protests, and the victories won by African Americans as well as by other minority groups and women. Baldwin himself confirmed this when, in his 1984 *Paris Review* interview, he admitted how much things have changed: "When I was a kid," he said, "the world was white . . . and now it is struggling to *remain* white—a very different thing." Similarly, in his essay "Stranger in the Village," he wrote, "The world is white no longer, and it will never be white again." Baba, many things have changed in America since you were here, but, unfortunately, some things have remained the same.

The backlash and violence we are facing today, as represented in Donald Trump and his Republican enablers, is due mainly to the fear that the weakening of racism and white power has incited, resulting in a strange alliance between the mainly white male establishment and the antiestablishment white supremacists who are on the fringes—a fear of the way that things are changing, as they use their full arsenal to try to cling to their power. The Republican Party has been on the defensive for a long time now, and the 2016 victory of Donald Trump and their kowtowing to the white supremacists and conspiracy theorists was an expression both of their fear and failure.

The truth is that even at the height of despair, Baldwin does not give up the struggle, and he acknowledges time and again that the struggle will not succeed without the participation of all races, and without the acceptance that race is an invention, a political construct. He has called white people "our stricken kinfolk," and he believes that we are all more connected than we recognize: "But we are all androgynous, not only because we are all born of a woman impregnated by the seed of man but because each of us, helplessly and forever, contains the other—male in female, female in male, white in black, and black in white. We are a part of each other." It is interesting that both Baldwin and Coates agree that race is a construct, a political ploy, but while Baldwin goes on to pathologize the white people ("our stricken kinfolk") who created this construct, Coates takes more of a "truth to power" approach, focusing on the political systems of subjugation erected upon the idea.

DEAR BABA, I WOKE UP today as if on the verge of a heart attack. I feel the same kind of anxiety I had felt back in the Islamic Republic: always on the alert, always waiting for bad news, and the pandemic creates the same kind of anxiety the war did, even during the times when everything seemed quiet. The other day, I woke up to the nightmare I used to have often: I had left home without my head cover and felt naked and exposed, expecting to be arrested at any moment.

I tried to calm myself, but watching the news on *Morning Joe* did not help, so I took my coffee and went out onto the balcony. Below me, the river, filled with green reflections, moved calmly. On the sidewalk, joggers and cyclists quietly passed by, but I didn't feel calm. It was as if the very air had become an invisible wall, making me feel claustrophobic.

I DON'T THINK THAT BALDWIN considered himself a revolutionary in the political sense of the word. The subversive, revolutionary nature of his work comes from his brilliance as a writer and not as a political activist. He is effective politically exactly because he comes from a different place; he looks at politics through new eyes. His vision endures not just because it's the opposite of the racist mindset, but also because it is so different from this mindset, woven from a different thread. It's a new way of perceiving the world and changing it. He claims, "You write in order to change the world, knowing perfectly well that you probably can't, but also knowing that literature is indispensable to the world. . . . The world changes according to the way people see it, and if you alter, even by a millimeter, the way people look at reality, then you can change it."

His writing is more dangerous than political—it is existential. The Irish writer Colm Toibin describes this so well in a thoughtful piece he wrote for the *London Review of Books* in 2001: "Baldwin wasn't really a political thinker, or even a novelist like Styron or Mailer whose work was fired by politics. . . . What makes his essays so compelling is that he insists on being personal, on forcing the public and the political to submit to his voice and the test of his experience and his observation." One more reason, Baba, I see such affinity between the way you both perceived the world and your own role in it.

Baldwin's writing was about his personal truth and trying to share that truth with others through his art. For him, the protest novel (the equivalent of the Socialist Realism novels you and I had so many problems with in Iran), "so far from disturbing, is an accepted and comforting aspect of the American scene, ramifying that framework we believe to be so necessary." He found the protest novel the opposite of revolutionary because it neatly categorizes everything and everyone, relieving us of ambiguities, contradictions, and complications, letting us bask in the knowledge that no matter what happens, the lines are drawn, and we are all safe as long as we don't cross them. Baldwin kept crossing the lines.

Dear Baba, the word *comforting* in the quote above is key here to one of the central problems that American society has faced throughout history: its desire for intellectual and spiritual comfort, its avoidance of pain at almost any cost. The constant need for entertainment, contempt for history, for thought, for reflection, the political and cultural polarizations and replacement of imagination and ideas with ideology are all rooted in this urge toward comfort. Baldwin was well aware of this; his writing reminds us of the necessity of confronting our true selves and facing pain and anguish rather than evading them.

This aversion to pain has now reached such epic proportions in America that we ban anything that is painful. In our classrooms, we teach our children to close their eyes to anything that pains them, to divert themselves from the bitterness of truth, to shield themselves with trigger warnings. We don't want to be disturbed. We might be able to ban fiction, but we cannot ban the realities of life, and life is filled with pain. If we don't confront these traumas, we are not really living. As Baldwin puts it, "I imagine that one of the reasons people cling to their hates so stubbornly is because they sense, once hate is gone that they will be forced to deal with pain."

There is, as Baldwin discovered, an invisible link between avoidance of pain and hate. Nowhere is this demonstrated better than in what goes by the name of identity politics, which appeases the desire for comfortable resolutions at both ends of the political spectrum, demonizing others, segregating them, and categorizing them. You are familiar with identity politics, which has been with us both on the Right and the Left, in one form or another, throughout history. But today, after Trump, it has gained dominance. We no longer need to engage genuinely with the other side or to deal with their or our own ambiguities and paradoxes. Coates describes it well: "Hate gives identity. The nigger, the fag, the bitch illuminate the border, illuminate what we ostensibly are not, illuminate the Dream of being white, of being a Man. We name the hated strangers and are thus confirmed in the tribe." Well, Baba jan, now this country has to face up to its pain—no more evasions.

WITH HIS WORK, BALDWIN MANAGED to do something else that few have done. Rather than shunning Western culture and the traditions associated with whiteness, he appropriated them, taking from the West the best it had to offer, the best any nation has to offer, its ideas and imagination. He mixed his legacy of jazz, folklore, and Negro spirituals with the Bible, Shakespeare, Henry James, Dickens, Dostoyevsky, Balzac, and Shaw. This mix created something original and uniquely Baldwinian and African American. Baldwin was not assimilated into the white culture, did not imitate or fawn over the white Western canon; instead, he took from it what he liked, what he needed, and then changed and redefined it by making it his own. This is literature at its best: a creative and empowering exchange with the other. With others.

I love Baldwin's 1964 essay "Why I Stopped Hating Shakespeare," which details how he came to appreciate and emulate Shakespeare's work. In one part, he talks about the English language and the fact that he initially felt alienated from it because it did not reflect his experiences. But he came to realize, "If the language was not my own, it might be the fault of the language; but it might also be my fault." He goes on to say that perhaps the language was not his because he had not tried to use it but had learned to only imitate it. He adds, "If this were so, then it might be made to bear the burden of my experience if I could find the stamina to challenge it, and me, to such a test." He says in support of this possibility that he had two "mighty witnesses:" his own "black ancestors, who evolved the sorrow songs, the blues, and jazz, and created an entirely new idiom in an overwhelmingly hostile place"—not to mention Shakespeare himself.

"Who is the Tolstoy of the Zulus, The Proust of the Papuans?" says Saul Bellow. "I'd be glad to read them." Coates in his book reminds us of Ralph Wiley, the sportswriter known for his literary tendencies and writings on race. Wiley, responding to Bellow, wryly remarked: "Tolstoy was the Tolstoy of the Zulus." He went on to say, "Unless you find a profit in fencing off universal properties of mankind into exclusive tribal ownership." In a single sentence, Wiley reminds us of the universality of ideas and imagination. Like scientific advances, they might originate at a specific place and time, but once they are out there in the world, they belong to the world—or, rather, belong to whoever cares about them, nurtures them, uses them. We need that imagination in order to survive as human beings. Where else but through imagination and ideas do we connect even with those we have never met in our lives?

I myself experienced the extraordinary role that stories

play in lives lived under extreme conditions. I have witnessed how imagination, ideas, and love of beauty open up spaces that reality closes to us. There is one story in particular that I cannot help repeating in my writing and my talks. I believe, however, that I never talked to you about it, Baba jan. It might be that you were traveling when it happened or that it hurt too much to talk about it then. I wrote about it in my diary instead, and later in a book of mine, but now I am telling it to you.

I want to talk to you about my student Razieh. I have talked and written about her before, but she doesn't go away. She keeps reappearing at different times and within different contexts, revealing new ideas and feelings, forcing me to return to her story. I have finally decided that for as long as she remains so strongly and vividly in my heart and mind, I will talk about her. Each time I do talk, there is something new to say, a context I had not noticed before. Razieh reminds me of everything that I hate in the Islamic Republic, for what they did to her and so many like her, and everything that I love in the Iranian people for how they resisted the regime's brutalities.

In my first year of teaching in the Islamic Republic of Iran, I taught at a girls' university and I had a student named Razieh whom I liked very much. She looked small and fragile but had a keen intelligence and a strong mind. Her father was dead and her mother was a cleaning woman. Both Razieh and her mother were very religious. Razieh belonged to the mujahedeen, an Islamic organization opposed to the Islamic regime. But she was never fanatically ideological. Razieh was loyal to her own principles and values, her own interpretation of her religion, and she was often critical of her group. What

always amazed me about Razieh was her insatiable passion
for beauty. She once told me how, as a child, her love of
books made her borrow and sometimes even steal from the
houses her mother worked in. She felt that no rich kid could
understand the value of those books the way she did. She read
Uncle Tom's Cabin and Daphne de Maurier's *Rebecca*. Later,
she fell for great fiction, for Tolstoy, Jane Austen, and Ernest
Hemingway, but her real passion was Henry James and what
she called his fiercely independent women. "James," she told
me, "he is so different from any other writer I have ever read."
Laughing, she added, "I think I am in love!"

At the end of the academic year, I left that university, and
except for one brief encounter in the street, I never saw Razieh
again. A few years later, another one of my students, whom I
had not seen for a long time, suddenly came to visit me. This
student I remembered as a bubbly, funny girl; now she was a
somber and subdued woman, pregnant with her second child.
She told me that during the student demonstrations against
the Cultural Revolution of the early 1980s, she had been
arrested and given five years in prison, though she was released
after two and half years for good behavior. I didn't ask her
what good behavior meant in her jailers' terms.

She continued, "While in jail, I met another student of
yours. There were fifteen of us in that cell. Her name was
Razieh." I forgot to ask her how she, a secular Marxist, was
in the same cell as Razieh, a militant Muslim. "Razieh," she
said, "told me about your classes on Hemingway and Henry
James, and I told her about *The Great Gatsby* and how in our
class we put the book on trial. We laughed a lot about that."
She paused, then said, "You know, soon after that, Razieh was
executed."

It took me a long time to get the meaning behind her words. I didn't ask her many questions. I could not imagine, or perhaps I did not want to imagine, that the slight, dark girl with fierce and determined eyes, that girl with such a glow in those eyes every time she talked of Henry James and Catherine Sloper, the protagonist of his novel *Washington Square*, was taken out one night and executed. I kept imagining Razieh laughing and saying, "I think I am in love!" Dear Baba, all I can do to keep her alive is repeat her story and remember her love affair with Henry James.

It occurs to me now that Razieh and Baldwin had Henry James in common. They both came from times and places vastly different from James's, yet connected to him in profound and intimate ways. You know, Baba, I think true equality is based on celebration and appreciation of difference, accompanied by the recognition and acceptance of the common spaces we share and the universality of humanity.

Razieh's story reminds me of Tzvetan Todorov's great book *Facing the Extreme*. He introduces us to Kostylev, a young Communist soldier, who, while browsing in a library, accidentally came across Flaubert's *Sentimental Education* and Benjamin Constant's *Adolphe*. Reading them preoccupied him to such a degree that he neglected his duties and was arrested. But he expressed no regrets, saying, "If I have ever known, even for a short time, what freedom is, it was when I was reading those old French books." The Dutch writer Etty Hillesum, a victim of the concentration camp, said, "A camp needs a poet, one who experiences life there, even there, as a bard and is able to sing about it." Telling about their lives in those death camps through stories or poetry was a way for the victims to take control of their confiscated lives; to tell their

stories from their own perspective and not the viewpoint of
their persecutors—you can say that under those circumstances
they read dangerously. It was through these accounts that they
connected to the world, that they made sure they were not
forgotten, for, yes, it is true that oblivion equals death.

You might say, Baba, that Henry James did not save my
student Razieh from execution. So what is it that makes so
many turn to ideas, imagination, and beauty when they have
been stripped of everything that we call life? When they
are so absolutely without power over their own lives and
deaths? When they are at death's door? When faced with such
extreme acts of brutality and inhumanity, when we lose hope
in being human, we instinctively turn to those achievements
of humanity that appreciate dignity, freedom, beauty. We turn
to empathy and the belief that even in such places so near to
death, we are also near to life through books, art, and music,
through what has been created out of love, passion, the desire
to connect, the urge to resist death and oblivion. As important
is the fact that even at death's door, when we cannot choose
the manner of our life or death, we still have the choice of *how*
to face that death, how to face our executioner: with dignity
and love of life or the void offered by death. We cannot lose
hope in a world that creates a Rumi or a Shakespeare.

I cannot imagine Razieh's execution, but I can imagine
her laughter with her cell mate and former classmate over
Fitzgerald and James. This, in the end, is what great stories
offer us: hope in the world despite all its evil and hope in
humanity despite all its flaws.

Baldwin's appreciation of great western fiction, like Razieh
and my other students' love for that literature, did not mean
that they were unaware of the West's flaws. In fact, some of

the best and most effective criticism of America and the West, which I talk about both in *Reading Lolita in Tehran* and *The Republic of Imagination*, comes from those works themselves.

Baba jan, I said this once during a panel discussion with Elias Khoury and Turkish journalist Ece Temelkuran, and Khoury told me, "But I want to tell you something very important: Henry James did not save Razieh. But Razieh saved Henry James." He said that "we writers don't save anybody." He added, "And if we are saved by them, [the readers], this is the magic of relationships between the reader and the words." Khoury also told us that the root of *word* in Arabic comes from another word: *wound*. I believe readers from different times and places, from different backgrounds, keep the books alive by reading them and redefining and reinterpreting them through their unique eyes. Razieh and Baldwin both give us different perspectives on James, making him relevant and resurrecting him in a new context.

BABA JAN, I BEGAN THESE letters with protests in Iran and now finish them with protests in America. A few days ago, Bijan and I participated in a demonstration. I was worried about his underlying condition, his cancer, but we both wanted to participate physically. We walked from our place to the White House, then followed those demonstrators moving toward the segment of Sixteenth Street that DC mayor Muriel Bowser had renamed Black Lives Matter Plaza. I thought of your friend the Black doorman at Blair House and how he probably would have felt at seeing the renamed plaza and the diverse crowd of demonstrators demanding the justice he had sought so many decades ago. At first, I was just walking alongside others, letting the mood of the place soak in. As I walked, I became more and more emotional, and teared up. I put on my sunglasses, so that others wouldn't notice. If I were asked why I was crying, I could not tell. Was it because I was afraid the glimmers of hope I was experiencing might turn into disillusion?

For a decade and half, I had written and talked about what I saw as a malaise taking over the United States, often wondering how people could become so complacent, so silent, even after Trump occupied the White House. Now, suddenly, the majority of Americans wanted change, and the young generation was demanding justice. Perhaps I worried that my hope might jinx progress. But this story is not finished— indeed, it is just beginning—and how it will develop depends on the attitudes of those who lead as well as those who participate in these protests. Will they offer a vision, a new way of looking at the world and changing it? Will they open new spaces, new ways of communicating?

Later, I reflected that perhaps my tears came from the fact that for three and a half years, Trump had taken away our ability to connect through curiosity and empathy. Using the virulent language of hate, he had left no room for love. The image of George Floyd and his words "I can't breathe" touched our hearts, and against the hatred handed out by Trump, it gave our hearts a reason to come to the forefront, to reject our own paralysis, to become not only human but humane once again. These protests are not merely political, they are protests of the heart and of the spirit.

I REALLY BELIEVE THAT BOOKS might not save us from death, but they help us live and live with hope, trying to link what Baldwin called "the possibilities of books" to the "impossibilities of life." For Baldwin, "Societies never know it, but the war of an artist with his society is a lover's war, and he does, at his best, what lovers do, which is to reveal the beloved to himself and, with that revelation, to make freedom real."

So you see, Baba jan, Baldwin teaches us the proximity of hope and pain, so that when I am faced with those checkpoint guys with their guns or the white nationalists with their semiautomatic rifles, I do not wish their guns were mine. Still, I win the fight.

With love
Baba's daughter,
Azi

CONCLUSION

Readers are born free and they ought to remain free.

—Vladimir Nabokov

WHEN IT COMES TO FREEDOM, writers and readers are joined at the hip, for the freedom of one guarantees that of the other. Writing, of course, may have repercussions for writers, placing them in danger, but books can also be dangerous for readers. Because great works of fiction are about revealing the truth, great writers, in this sense, become witnesses to the truth; they do not, *cannot*, remain silent. But readers, as well, once they read the work, cannot remain silent either. This is true especially now.

I speak here not only as a writer and a reader but also as a parent and grandparent. Ever since August 2020, a month in which my two grandchildren, Iliana and Cyrus, were born, even more than before, I ask myself what kind of a world are we leaving behind for our children and grandchildren? Being born in such turbulent times, polarized times, when the focus is on the conflict with those we label our enemies, I want them to know about their migrant legacy. I want them to know that our family came to this country in search of freedom and because of freedom, and, once in this country, we became involved in defending that freedom—not just from outside enemies but, even more dangerous, from those within. I want to provide them with a portable home like the one my father gave me: one place where they will feel completely free and one that no one on earth can take away from them.

Readers, of course, have no formal organization to promote truth, to bring about change. But they number in the billions. They range across the spectrums of profession, background, gender, race, ethnicity, religious affiliation. Collectively, their power would be immense. Every writer who is censored, jailed, or tortured and murdered; every reader who is deprived of reading the books she wants; every bookstore, library, museum, or theater that closes; every book that is censored or removed from schools and libraries; every art, music, or literature program canceled in our schools and other institutions—these should all remind us of our responsibility.

My dear fellow reader, in a world made opaque by wars and conflict, one in which our enemies may dominate our hearts and minds more than our friends do, where lies masquerade as truth, we need the clear eyes of imagination to see the reality behind and beyond the show. Which is why, although I try to avoid slogans, I am going to end this book with one:

Readers of the World, Unite!

ACKNOWLEDGMENTS

READ DANGEROUSLY IS IN MANY ways the last in a quartet of books, which, setting aside my memoir *Things I Have Been Silent About*, began with *That Other World, Reading Lolita in Tehran,* and *The Republic of Imagination.* This provides me with an opportunity to thank those who, in various ways, have supported me throughout the writing of some or all of these books.

First and foremost: my husband, best friend, and critic, Bijan, and our children, Negar and Dara Naderi, for their love, interest, support, and sense of humor. I benefited a great deal from discussions with Negar and Dara, along with their spouses, Jason Guedenis and Kelli Colman, about the main themes in this book. Negar and I had many conversations about this book and her memories of my father—thank you, Negar jan. My grandchildren, Iliana Nafisi Guedenis and Cyrus Colman Naderi, thank you, thank you, and thank you! In memory of Bryce Nafisi Naderi, my silent and constant companion throughout the writing of this and my other books.

My thanks as always to Andrew Wylie for his constant and consistent support, and his colleagues at the Wylie Agency, especially my thoughtful and gracious agent, Sarah Chalfant, for her friendship, her great advice, and her full commitment to her authors and books, literature in particular. My gratitude also to Charles Buchan for his support and friendship. Sarah Watling, thank you for your support throughout the writing of this book.

I would be remiss not to thank my lecture agent and my good

and trusted friend Steven Barclay and his colleagues at the Barclay Agency, especially Eliza Fischer, for continuous support and friendship. Steven saw me through some of the most difficult patches while writing this book. Steven, with you I always feel at home—thank you!

Thanks to my editor, Nick Amphlett, for his valuable suggestions, meticulous observations, patience, and all-around support. With Nick, I know my book is in great hands. Thank you to Jessica Sindler, who was my editor before she left for another job, for her support and belief in this book. Thank you to my colleagues at Dey Street, especially Liate Stehlik (president and publisher); Ben Steinberg (vice president and associate publisher); Carrie Thornton (vice president and editorial director); Emma Gordon and Ali Hinchcliffe (publicity); Anna Brill and Kell Wilson (marketing); and Jessica Rozler (production editor).

Mahnaz Afkhami, president and founder of Women's Learning Partnership, has supported my work since I wrote the first book of the quartet, *That Other World*, in Persian. When I decided to resign from my job at Allameh Tabatabai University to create a private class with my own curriculum and students, I discussed this idea with some colleagues and friends, most of whom told me that it would fail. Mahnaz, on the other hand, was both encouraging and enthusiastic, and showed her support by offering me a grant from her organization Sisterhood Is Global. As the minister for Women's Affairs during the Pahlavi era, she also shared with me insights into the advances in women's rights at that time and how those achievements nourished women's current struggles against the Islamic Republic's repressive laws.

Joanne Leedom-Ackerman has supported my writing from the first time I talked to her about writing *Reading Lolita in Tehran*. We had many discussions about this book, and she, apart from my husband, Bijan, was the only one who read the full manuscript, offering great comments. On another note, Joanne, thank you for reminding me of the inner voice and the Yasso bars!

I discussed the idea for this book with Ladan Boroumand. The idea of writing letters to my father was inspired by one of these discussions. Thank you, Ladan.

My thanks to the following friends for their friendship and support: the friend named "Shirin" in the book; Massumeh Farhad, Shahran Tabari, Abdi Nafisi, Sophie Benini Pietromarchi, Roya Boroumand, Stanley Staniski, and Naghmeh Zarbafian; and thank you, Naghmeh, for your translation of my father's letter to President Johnson.

Big thanks to my wonderful assistant, Amanda Taheri, for her enthusiasm and support. She helped me in research for this book, managed my social media, and helped keep me on schedule.

My Italian publisher at Adelphi, the late Roberto Calasso, was very enthusiastic about this book. We spent a whole evening over dinner with him and Sophie Benini Pietromarchi discussing it. I miss him and those marvelous discussions we had over the years since Adelphi published *Reading Lolita in Tehran* and my subsequent books.

I was offered a centennial fellowship at Georgetown's Edmund A. Walsh School of Foreign Service for the academic term of 2019. I would like to thank the dean of the School of Foreign Service, Dr. Joel Hellman; Professor Anthony Arend, chair of the Department of Government; and Claire Ogden. My special thanks to the junior fellows, the students who were assigned to help me with research on my book. We had great discussions and they enthusiastically helped with this research. I want to acknowledge Varsha Thebo, Youssef Osman, Grace Kim, and Rita Housseiny for their support. Rita Housseiny deserves a special thanks for continuing to help me beyond the duration of the fellowship and for her commitment to ideas and imagination.

Thanks to the Laboratory for Global Performance and Politics at the Georgetown University and its cofounders, Ambassador Cynthia Schneider and Derek Goldman, in whom I discovered kindred spirits committed to both works of imagination and social justice.

Some of my best memories about the writing of this book belong to my fellowship at Civitella Ranieri Foundation, where my daily contact with a group of artists and writers created the best inspiration for writing. My thanks to Dana Prescott and her great team at Civitella.

MY FATHER'S LETTER TO LYNDON B. JOHNSON

HERE IS THE FULL TEXT of the letter my father wrote from jail to Lyndon Johnson, which I reference in my letters to my father in this book.

Mr. President,

The US presidential election results are not clear yet and no one can be certain about its fate. The writer of this letter is an individual who, in the words of Daniel Webster, has "resolved to push [his] skiff from the shore alone" into an adverse and turbulent sea while knowing how hard it is to do so. I have seen a paradise called America and the promised land of Texas. I am well aware of the hell of Hiroshima, vortex of Vietnam, sinkhole of the Middle East, and wish that the candidate who wins the election to be the very person who—like Franklin Roosevelt—believes "the only thing we have to fear is fear itself"; the very person who says we should build "an America in which every citizen shares all the opportunities of his society, in which every man has a chance to advance his welfare to the limit of his capacities"; the very person who writes that our brains—as our hearts—tell us we should try to make a better world; the very person who pursues this goal: a richer life for each and every woman, man, and child; and believes that one should help those who need training and education or want jobs and salaries to make ends meet for themselves and their families; above all, the very person who wants to "give every citizen an escape from the crushing weight of poverty." The writer of this letter thinks that the winner of the election must be the same person who believes that our society should be a place where we can remove the dark shadow of war and suspicion from our nations and our families; a society in which every citizen is granted "the full equality which God enjoins and the law requires, whatever his belief, or race, or the color of his skin"; a society in which Americans can become not only richer and stronger, but happier and wiser. I believe that the winner of the election should be the one who thinks "our material progress is only the foundation on which we will build a richer life of mind and spirit"; and finally, the one who says: "The Great Society is a place where every child can find knowledge to enrich his mind and to enlarge his talents. It is a place where leisure is a welcome chance to build and reflect, not a feared cause of boredom and restlessness. It is a place where the city of man serves not only the needs of the body and the demands of commerce but the desire for beauty and the hunger for community." It is such a person who should be victorious in the election, not his rival whose reaction to the frustrated individuals rebelling against oppression, tyranny, and poverty is a nuclear bomb; or who wishes to maintain the legacy of slavery and racial discrimination in the name of defending freedom and people's honor.

I have seen the anxiety and agitation of striking workers in Detroit, watching them in deep distress lying along streets

with bottles of whiskey in their hands; I have observed
the worn-out, sad, wistful residents of the ruined, grimy
buildings covered with broken windows in Harlem and the
Black neighborhoods of Chicago; I have empathized with
America's castaway people of color on the Nineteenth Street
of Washington; I have witnessed the sorrowful faces of
the hungry, jobless workers on the docksides of New York,
Baltimore, and New Orleans. Yet, I have also passed by the
newly constructed buildings whose doors open automatically in
front of people and whose façade, as well as internal facilities,
signify their owners' utmost comfort and well-being; I have
enjoyed the infinite blessings of individual freedom in your
land and relished the beautiful parks, luxurious theaters,
magnificent restaurants, excellent cars, and airplanes, as well
as the comfortable life in your country—and having witnessed
all those, I am very much eager to see the person whose
thoughts I briefly recounted here win the election.

As a person who is interested in the fate of the civilized
world and thinks that your decisions would affect his own
country, I wish you success. Although I am not an American
voter, I would like to remind you that you do not merely
need your own people's votes today. Given the extent of the
US foreign policy all over the world, people's votes in other
countries unofficially create different impacts on the political
policies of this country. It should be noted, however, that
it is still the financial and domestic economic policies that
would determine your fate for the following reasons: First,
domestic products are mostly consumed in the country;
second, the volume of exports are much less than domestic
consumptions. Therefore, your foreign policy might be of
secondary importance. Or the United States—because of its

current power and capabilities—might have closed its eyes
to the issues of other countries. Nonetheless, you should
know that these days other countries play more roles in your
decisions and you will have to pay more attention to them as
well as their needs and policies: American voters might one
day ask why the taxes they pay are spent on wars overseas or
why young Americans are killed in Indochina. Today, cartels,
companies, and owners of large industries ask you the same
question or somehow get the government involved for their
own interests. Tomorrow, ordinary Americans will get curious
about this issue and if you do not come up with suitable
answers to their questions, you should expect to lose their
positive votes.

One day soon you will no longer think that the privileges
of civilization exclusively belong to American people. In order
to maintain economic balance and sustain welfare, you will
have to export freedom, political immunity, jobs, bread and
culture to other countries—instead of jazz, variety of dances,
opposition to traditions and disintegration of the family
unit. One day soon you will have to recognize equality and
brotherhood in political exchanges as the right of all people
in the world. And instead of sending the John Birch Society
agenda or the US surplus of suits, wheat, gums and candies to
them as an act of charity, you will have to extend the hand of
empathy to them.

Mr. Johnson, America is in debt to other nations for two
reasons: First, as you once said, it is the natural duty of a
person who enjoys more divine gifts to help others; therefore,
you—as the wealthier brother of mankind—should take a
step to respect them and contribute to their progress, thereby

maintaining your own prominence and wealth This needs
to be done, however, not as an act of charity or some sort of
patronization but in gratitude for the natural gift granted to
you. The second reason is that other nations have provided
your country with their natural wealth—which is their major
asset--or contributed to the development of your goals with
their lives and wealth.

My advice to you is:

1. TRY TO BE A "POLITICIAN," but not in the Eastern or Western
sense of the word. A politician, in the Eastern sense of the
word, is someone who finds himself weak in the face of the
great powers, acting as a sheep that does not want to surrender
to a wolf. This kind of politician resorts to telling lies to
hide his weakness in front of his people so much so that you
can seldom find a politician who is not a liar; this despicable
quality has indeed become synonymous with politics. Politics,
in the Western sense of the word, is believing in Frank
Kent's statement: one cannot call a political profession an
unethical job; we can only say that politics is not an ethical
profession. Apparently, the greatest art of a Western political
man is the ability to say one thing and do another. In fact,
it is not important if he takes the right side insofar as he
temporarily takes people's side. Fortunately, the American
nation, throughout the short history of their country, has
not supported such a professional politician for a long time.
John Quincy Adams, who passionately endorsed President
Jefferson's Embargo Act, and Daniel Webster, who saved the
national unity by his speech to the Senate on March 7, 1850—
for which his rivals condemned him for as long as he lived—

were the best and bravest men of your history. Fortunately, your country's political tradition frees congressmen from obligations and leaves them to their own conscience. Consequently, unlike many other countries, congressmen or senators do not see themselves indebted to their voters or act as their private attorneys. Neither do people expect them to act against their conscience or free will. Moreover, in your country, moral courage always goes hand in hand with other excellent traits such as righteousness, sincerity, and power of decision making. To American people, moral integrity of their political elite is far more important than vastness of their knowledge and thought. As Professor Allan Nevins once noted, George Washington won the American Revolutionary War because of his moral principles, not his intelligence or wisdom. In the same vein, it was Lincoln's morals that kept the national unity during the American Civil War, not his knowledge. You should not overlook virtue or ignore the interests of the majority merely to satisfy a certain group. Of course, the weakness of democracy is that it yields to public demand and pays bribes to gain votes. For some politicians, unfortunately, maintaining the interests of the majority is not essential; their interest lies in satisfying the yes men and influential voters.

As the leader of a free nation, you should neither compromise over the interests of other small nations nor do business with the heads of opposing forces over other countries' independence, honor of their leaders and freedom of their people. As John Bright says, political men should not be called "great politicians" simply because they occupy key positions in their lives; in order to acquire that title, they must possess the virtue of greatness and spirituality. If you want to remain a great man and an eminent politician in the US history, you should pay attention not only to American voters but to the votes and ideas of people in other countries. The previous US presidents, except for the last three ones, were never put through such a test. Your non-isolation, all-embracing policy has now come to fruition, making you worthy of a global title.

2. MY SECOND ADVICE TO YOU IS: Try not to fall into traps of other countries' politicians. Particularly, be on guard against those weak individuals who try to befriend you in different ways as soon as they see your abundance of "might and money." They often approach your novice political or military representatives at dinner parties or soirees, seeking collaboration with them while showing a kind of humility typical of weak individuals. It is then that the waves of recommendations start pouring into the White House, making you fall into traps of personal and moral commitments unwillingly. As a result, other nations' freedom and prosperity would be sacrificed for the worthless, ambitious, false intentions of those whose only merit is speaking English with an American accent; those whose only talent is to deceive your naïve officials. Many a free nation has been thrown into others' traps in this fashion! Many a nation, worthy of democracy and law, has been thrown into the opposite direction! You can see such political games in Cuba. The tyrannous, oppressive, corrupt government of Batista enjoyed no support but from your officials—the outcome of which was Castro who flirted with a group of your officials. Then, upon rising to power with their help, he became unfaithful and turned into a dangerous ulcer in the US neighborhood. There were also other cases

such as what happened in Indochina and Vietnam: One day, a number of reports provoked the White House to advocate Ngo Dinh Diem while making the biased Buddhists set themselves on fire. It was not until the smell of smoke from their leaders' burned bodies and the muffled cries from their despondent followers filled the air that your feelings were evoked. One million displaced Catholics are anxiously watching General Khanh lest he shares the same fate of his predecessors. Why aren't there any conflicts between Catholics and Buddhists in North Vietnam? Do you think they are really Communists? Most of them, both in North and South, are struggling to find a loaf of bread not to starve. A hungry stomach has no faith. The difference between North and South is that people in South Vietnam have tested the rulers who are all birds of a feather and lost their hope in them. However, they have not yet tested the Communist northerners—the newcomers who promise a different kind of heaven, their words and actions are different, more practical, this worldly and without any empty promises. American money, equipment, and soldiers are everywhere; however, it would be better if this money were spent on nurturing talents and improving the public welfare: the war would have ended, and people would have started to build up their land. In the Middle East, too, you were entangled in a snare of ambitious individuals with different titles and in opposition to one another—all of whom under your endorsement. In Egypt, its leader claims to be the king of the world with your officials' support, desiring to bring all—from Yemen to Egypt and from Muscat to Beirut—under his own flag. If one can claim a land merely based on race or language, why don't you conquer Australia, India, England and other English-speaking countries? Your divine mission in the great society should be to save people of the world from anxiety. It is far from sufficient if you fight with a giant called Communism or set up an army for peace and against poverty. Launch an army for dispelling anxiety instead and stop petty leeches from sucking people's blood. Seek the truth sincerely, so that each nation within the framework of its own country can enjoy the divine blessings. And if they are not talented enough to do so, send advocates of peace and freedom to teach them the ways of democracy.

Fight with tyrants, big or small, everywhere. Remember John Stuart Mill's rationale for fighting against the tyranny of British military rule in Jamaica. He said he was not doing it out of pity for the Blacks in that country but mostly for maintaining the principles of democracy. "The question was, whether the British dependencies, and eventually perhaps Great Britain itself, were to be under the government of law, or of military license," said Mill. You, too, can treat everyone equally and avoid trying to export "fledgling Americans" to other countries. People of India do not approve of your tall stature and masculine face; they love their own Gandhi. You, too, can love their dear Gandhi and find a way to their hearts accordingly! Do not rely on someone merely because they received their education in the United States or were approved by your officials. This is not what true, righteous leaders do; this is rather what professional politicians do—those who lie not only to you but to their own nations. They are so ignorant and weak that they would either imprison or deprive of political life all those who might follow your right path on the pretext of espionage, defamation, or libel. Thus doing, they themselves will turn into double agents—which is far more dangerous than any other danger. Why should America in all its grandeur get involved in such affairs? Why does your country—which was a colony and freed itself from the yoke of subjugation by sacrificing lives—follow the colonialists in brainwashing and ruling the minds of idiots? Know that this path leads but to a dead end.

3. DO NOT THINK THAT ANYONE who takes a path different from that of yours is your enemy. Life is not black and white; even if it is so, one complements—not opposes—the other. The path of truth is one, albeit human beings have different perceptions of it, their ways of thinking are different, and they express themselves differently. A single thought can be manifested variously when conveyed in various forms of words. Any moderate man deserves freedom. Freedom constitutes progress. When a man is in chains and ruled, his mind never flourishes; his innate ability never develops. This assumption that "whoever is not with us is against us"— which has dominated the American mind for a long time—is totally wrong. Why do you fear Communism? Scientific Communism would not pose any problems for anyone. We might not like the Soviet Union's governance system, but this cannot be a justification for rejecting Communists. People have different perceptions in different parts of the world. How many talented people have you chained up in the name of Communism? In a country like America where prosperity exists, opportunity to study is provided, jobs abound, and the rule of law reigns, Communism cannot grow, especially in its current form. Stripped of its philosophical nature, Communism has now divided human beings into two classes of employers and workers in the name of proletariat. Not to mention that it has already been put to test—the result of

which is quite evident in its own birthplace. Communism is not to be feared. Remember the words of the late Indian prime minister Jawaharlal Nehru, whom you once cited yourself: Not merely two contradictory economic views— capitalism and socialism—exist in the world and not merely these two views can exclusively address economic production and distribution. In Nehru's opinion, one can easily reach a middle path drawn from the ideals of both the socialist and capitalist economies, whose result can be a moderate, more suitable system. Rest assured that the India built by Gandhi and Nehru is much more useful for the free world than other governments such as those of Vietnam, Laos, and the like. Others have their own ways. And you do not want anything but spreading freedom, establishing democracy, uprooting poverty, and promoting reconciliation between nations, do you?

4. MY LAST ADVICE TO YOU IS to avoid giving any kinds of charity, whether state or national, to other nations. Even if you do help others, it should be based on the principles in which you believe and according to which you act. Otherwise, an honorable individual would not be patronized even when in need—he might accept your money and spend it but would not remain grateful for it. One of your fruitful post–World War II assistance plans was the Marshall Plan for reconstructing Europe that pushed this war-ridden, destitute continent towards recovery and progress. The outcome of that plan was an improvement in economic conditions, production, and reconstructions of ruins of war. Through the efforts of war-torn people and considerable funds from the United States, the damages of war were repaired in no

time and rapid progress was made in science and technology. After all, Europeans are your grandparents and this young tree called America has been irrigated by the blood of their young and old. Nonetheless, other plans such as Truman's Point Four Program in Asia and Africa as well as Marshall Plan in China achieved no results. All the money and weapons used in China emerged somehow in the enemies' arsenal. The implementation of the Point Four Program in Iran brought neither prosperity to us, nor glory to you. Not to mention, it even created an Americanized class who occupied all the government's strategic positions as long as they were under your protection. And as soon as the dragon of the revolution stuck its fiery tongue out, each and every one of them escaped to a corner—under the protection of the superpower—to regret all the good tasks they had not undertaken, although I doubt that they were even honorable enough to truly feel such regrets. During the same time that Mr. Warne was in charge of the Point Four Program in Iran (and I had a share of its educational scholarships myself), I wrote a letter saying the Iranians concerned about their own country have questions about the $10 to $12 million spent to implement the program. I wrote that it would be futile both for the United States and the Iranian people if the objective of this program was simply to pay some individuals to perform a number of small tasks which would be of no use to anyone. If you wish to do a profitable and enduring job with this money, you can either do only one project but do it thoroughly or choose one Iranian province and launch several worthwhile projects there. For instance, spend the entire money on Iranians' health care and building hospitals throughout the year. Thus doing, you will leave a good name behind and the whole country will always know and appreciate your service. You can also take one province, say Kerman, to discover and extract its mines, improve its agriculture by cultivating dates, pistachios, and henna, or combat malaria and its other local diseases. Then you can see how the people of this country will always remember America for its benevolence. The day I went to the Point Four Organization, located on the intersection of Sepah and Pahlavi streets in Tehran, it felt like I had entered into an American institution: the only language spoken there was American English, and the only method used, an American one. Upon meeting me, Mr. Warne, who was one and a half times taller than me, stood up from behind a desk which was twice the size of our prime minister's desk, and sat beside me on a bench. He said: I had never heard what you wrote in your letter from any Iranians before. I said: I'm not an imitator; I'm an innovator. If anyone had written those words before, there would inevitably be some reactions. He said: What you wrote is true, but we don't plan to stay here for years and most of the budget we have is to be spent on Iranians' salaries. I asked: What is the output of $1 million-a-month salary? He said: Review, statistics and research. I said: What do you do with the statistics and review results? He said: It is used at government offices as well as for research and analysis. At the end, he said: Such plans show the extent of America's interest in the Iranian people. I said: Which of the plans whose efficacy is proven have been implemented? He replied with a triumphant smile: The plan to combat malaria, especially in northern Iran and other places. I said: That is correct. This plan deserves to be embraced; I wish you had spent all your money on such plans—it would have made us happy and you, successful . . .

Mr. President, you are in no debt to anyone. However, as I mentioned earlier in this letter, you enjoy more divine blessings, to say nothing of the fact that you are far from the international battlefields. For that reason, you owe other countries, including Iran. By loving your neighbors, you demonstrate your love for God. But know that if you do things out of mere "charity," it violates the legal rights of human beings and wounds their self-esteem.

In conclusion, I wish you success in the election and admire the great American nation, who has amazed everyone with their scientific and technological advances. Lawfulness as well as freedom of thought and action have benefited both you and the world. I hope that other countries of the world, too, can follow in your footsteps in scientific progress, respect for freedom, human rights, and law.

Mr. President, as the late Senator Taft says, freedom of thought and opinion is a blessing that everyone should enjoy. Freedom should not be exclusive; neither should it be exported. Freedom should rather be taught, and one should learn how to obtain it. Only a powerful politician like Edmund Ross could "look down into [his] open grave" to save Andrew Johnson, your namesake. Only he, by making such a sacrifice, could lead America into a course whose outcome we can witness now. The national hero of Texas Sam Houston once said: "I wish no prouder epitaph to mark the board or slab that may lie on my tomb than this: 'He loved his country, he was a patriot; he was devoted to the Union.'" I hope that one day, after a hundred years, they write on your headstone: "This man loved human beings and worshipped his country; he was truly devoted to Americans and humanity."

May John F. Kennedy—whose assassination moved the whole world into tears—rest in peace! He was the one who introduced you, his honest and humanitarian colleague, to the world. I wish you luck!

—An ordinary Iranian who wants everyone to equally enjoy the blessings of liberty, equality and fraternity while being grateful only to God!
Detention Center of Iran's Justice Department, 1966

Translated by Naghmeh Zarbafian

BOOKS REFERENCED

ACKERMAN, ELLIOT. *Green on Blue*. Scribner, 2016.

ACKERMAN, ELLIOT. *Places and Names: On War, Revolution, and Returning*. Penguin Press, 2019.

ACKERMAN, ELLIOT, AND JAMES STAVRIDIS. *2034: A Novel of the Next World War*. Penguin Press, 2021.

ATWOOD, MARGARET. *The Blind Assassin*. Anchor Books/Random House, 2001.

ATWOOD, MARGARET. *The Handmaid's Tale*. Anchor Books, 1998.

ATWOOD, MARGARET. *Moving Targets: Writing with Intent 1982–2004*. House of Anansi Press, 2004.

ATWOOD, MARGARET. *Negotiating with the Dead: A Writer on Writing*. Cambridge University Press, 2002.

ATWOOD, MARGARET. *The Testaments*. Nan A. Talese/Doubleday, 2019.

BALDWIN, JAMES. *Another Country*. Vintage Books, 1992.

BALDWIN, JAMES. *Giovanni's Room*. Vintage Books, 2013.

BALDWIN, JAMES. *Go Tell It on the Mountain*. Vintage International, 2013.

BALDWIN, JAMES. *No Name in the Street*. The Dial Press, 1972.

BALDWIN, JAMES. *Notes of a Native Son*. Beacon Press, 2012.

BALDWIN, JAMES. *The Fire Next Time*. Vintage, 1992.

BALDWIN, JAMES. *The Price of the Ticket*. St. Martin's Press, 1985.

BALDWIN, JAMES, AND MARGARET MEAD. *A Rap on Race*. J. B. Lippincott, 1971.

BOYD, VALERIE. *Wrapped in Rainbows: The Life of Zora Neale Hurston*. Scribner, 2004.

BRADBURY, RAY. *Fahrenheit 451*. Random House, 1953.

COATES, TA-NEHISI. *Between the World and Me*. Spiegel & Grau, 2015.

FERDOWSI, ABOLQASEM. *Shahnameh: The Persian Book of Kings*. Translated by Dick Davis, Penguin Classics, 2016.

FIELD, DOUGLAS. *James Baldwin*. Liverpool University Press, 2011.

GLAUDE JR., EDDIE S. *Begin Again: James Baldwin's America and Its Urgent Lessons for Our Own*. Crown, 2020.

GROSSMAN, DAVID. *Falling Out of Time*. Translated by Jessica Cohen, Knopf, 2014.

GROSSMAN, DAVID. *To The End of the Land*. Vintage International, 2011.

GROSSMAN, DAVID. *Writing in the Dark: Essays on Literature and Politics*. Translated by Jessica Cohen, Farrar, Straus and Giroux, 2008.

HURSTON, ZORA NEALE. *Dust Tracks on the Road: An Autobiography*. J. B. Lippincott, 1942.

HURSTON, ZORA NEALE. *Moses, Man of the Mountain*. Amistad, 2008.

HURSTON, ZORA NEALE. *Their Eyes Were Watching God*. J. B. Lippincott, 1937.

KHOURY, ELIAS. *Gate of the Sun*. Picador, 2007.

LEEMING, DAVID. *James Baldwin: A Biography*. Arcade, 2015.

MORRISON, TONI. *Beloved*. Knopf, 1987.

MORRISON, TONI. *Burn This Book: PEN Writers Speak Out on the Power of the Word*. HarperStudio, 2009.

MORRISON, TONI. *The Bluest Eye*. Holt, Rinehart and Winston, 1970.

MORRISON, TONI. *The Dancing Mind*. Knopf, 1996.

MORRISON, TONI. *The Source of Self-Regard: Selected Essays, Speeches, and Meditations*. Knopf, 2019.

PARSIPUR, SHAHRNUSH. *Kissing the Sword: A Prison Memoir*. Translated by Sara Khalili, The Feminist Press, 2013.

PARSIPUR, SHAHRNUSH. *Women Without Men: A Novel of Modern Iran*. The Feminist Press, 2011.

PLATO. *The Republic*. Translated by Desmond Lee, Penguin Classics, 2007.

RAVANIPOUR, MONIRO. *The Drowned*. Translated by M. R. Ghanoonparvar, 2019.

RUSHDIE, SALMAN. *Imaginary Homelands: Essays and Criticism 1981–1991*. Penguin Books, 1992.

RUSHDIE, SALMAN. *Midnight's Children*. Jonathan Cape, 1981.

RUSHDIE, SALMAN. *Step Across This Line: Collected Nonfiction 1992–2002*. Modern Library, 2003.

RUSHDIE, SALMAN. *The Satanic Verses*. Henry Holt & Co, 1997.

TODOROV, TZVETAN. *Facing the Extreme: Moral Life in the Concentration Camps*. Henry Holt & Co, 1996.